Dana has written a comprehensive and hi
heart of our loving and communicating Cr
every illustration is full of God's life-giving

You cannot read this without an amazing conclusion that God had written a
tremendous book, but has never stopped talking!
So, read Dana's book, be equipped, be encouraged, and be activated into a
fresh revelation of your relationship with a "talking God" who loves you and
will use you to speak His thoughts to the world you live in.

Dr. Clem Ferris

I have known Dana and Cheryl Easterling for quite a few years now. Certain
words come to mind when I consider Dana and Cheryl. Passion. Devotion.
Commitment. Tenacity. Strength, of mind, of character, of joy. Energy.
Compassion. Integrity. Determination, to see Father God glorified. Tireless, in
preparing the saints for the work of the ministry. Those characteristics are
painted into every page of Dana's new book, The Prophetic Expression. This
book presents a clear, concise and uncomplicated look at the reality of the
prophetic expression as it should be -- must be -- in the lives of God's children
and in the everyday life of the church. Dana's presentation, with plenty of
real life illustrations, will give you a dependable road map for understanding
and developing the prophetic expression in the local church. Read It!

Bryan L. Asay, Bozeman, Montana
Attorney and former senior leader of Mount Helena Community Church,
Helena Montana

Reading The Prophetic Expression is much like having a conversation with its
author, Dana Easterling; you always come away built up, encouraged and
more equipped spiritually to be who you were created to be. Biblically sound,
easy to understand, and wonderfully practical, each page invites you to step
in to the prophetic and express the heart of God. All who desire to be used by
God to bless others will learn from and love this book.

David Kobelin, Pastor, Professional Life Coach, Awyken Master Coach Trainer

The Prophetic Expression is a very helpful read. Especially in the areas of understanding the heart of God to communicate with mankind. And to be able to decipher the difference between what is of the Spirit and what is from our own thinking, Thank you for getting the truth out for all to enjoy.

Pastor Duane Weinmeister, Senior Pastor, Boulder Assembly of God

The prophetic methodology that Dana shares in this book is tried and true. With a focus on the heart of God for His people, it allows prophetic ministry to take place in a safe and encouraging manner, for both those receiving and those giving ministry. Our team uses this approach to prophecy with great success!

Jen Rebo, Church Prophetic Ministry Leader

HEARING GOD'S VOICE FOR YOURSELF AND OTHERS

THE PROPHETIC EXPRESSION

DANA EASTERLING

The Prophetic Expression

Copyright © 2016 Dana Easterling

Requests for information should be addressed to:

Dana or Cheryl Easterling 2danaeast@gmail.com

Cover design: Jeff Wald

Printed in the United States of America

To my dear wife, Cheryl, You have been my faithful companion, a great friend and wife. For my children Mary, Nathan, Silas and Reece, I love each one of you more than you will ever know. You are a treasure to me. To the grandchildren I currently have and those yet to be born. I love every one of you. My wonderful family, you have added more to my life than I could have dreamed or asked for.

For all the friends that have been kind enough to share their lives with me. You helped shape me into who I am today, which in turn made this book a reality.

Contents

INTRODUCTION

The journey to writing this book on prophecy has been quite the long and winding road. As a young believer in a mainline denomination, I was taught that certain gifts and expressions presented in the Bible were only for the early church and not for Christians today. They were to help the Church become established during the time of the first Apostles and shortly thereafter. The expression of prophecy was one item on that list that had ceased to be a part of our *now* Christian experience. I received this teaching at face value, trusting my pastor's word. After all, he cared about me and had been a Christian longer.

However, as time passed and I grew in the Lord, I began seeing that the Bible clearly says in many places that prophecy is still for His church today. So my wife and I came out of that denomination and continued to walk the path the Lord was leading us on. That was over 25 years ago, and through these years we have witnessed much good, some not so good, and some harmful prophetic ministry. The goal of this book is to present a biblical foundation of prophetic expression. While this book focuses on hearing God's voice for yourself and others, you will also see a theme throughout of building and maintaining a solid Christ-centered life. Keeping Jesus first is our greatest joy. This close relationship with Him produces the purity in us that the Holy Spirit will use for a truly pure expression of God through us.

You will see as you read this book that there are lots of scripture references. Please use your Bible along with this book to see for yourself like the people of Berea did in (Acts 17:10-11) if these things are so. Always be diligent to build your life on God's written word, the Bible. It is my prayer that this book will increase your intimacy with our Lord, add strength to your life and beauty to His expression through you.

CHAPTER 1

God Speaks to His Children

The Last Days

Let's begin by looking at the time in history we live in. This will not be a natural History lesson, but a Biblical view. As we look at this, know that God could have placed you and me at any point in history, but He chose, I believe, the very best time for each one of us to live. In the Bible, there are four distinct periods of history spoken of. These are referred to as *Dispensations* or *Ages*. These four Ages show us how God deals with mankind, the way He interacts with people, God's requirements of people and their responsibilities to Him and to each other.

• The first dispensation *Age* was from Adam to Moses.

"The Patriarchs"

[14] Nevertheless, death reigned from Adam until Moses, even over those who had not sinned in the likeness of the offense of Adam, who is a [a]type of

13

Him who was to come.
-Romans 5:14 (NASB)

• The second *Age* was from Moses to John the Baptist.

"The Law"

13 For all the prophets and the Law prophesied until John.
-Matthew 11:13 (NASB)

• The third *Age* is the time between Jesus' first coming and His second coming.

"Grace"

[20] and that He may send [to you] Jesus, the Christ, who has been appointed for you, [21] whom heaven must keep until the time for the [complete] restoration of all things about which God promised through the mouth of His holy prophets from ancient time.
-Acts 3:20-21 (AMP)

• The fourth is the *Kingdom Age,* The time between the second coming of Christ and the end of the Kingdom age.

-See Revelation chapter 20

While each dispensation has some unique expressions and interactions between God and people, the Bible itself separates these four periods of time into specific *Ages* or *dispensations.* You are probably thinking by now, what does this have to do with prophecy? Actually, a lot, the reason is to present a clear biblical precedent for prophecy today. When we read in the Bible that God has something for us that is relevant for our lives today, we really, really need it. God does not waste His time or ours. When the Bible clearly says something, we are to study it, believe it, and plant His word deep into the soil of our hearts. His word contains all the power needed to express itself in us and through us.

You and I live in the third dispensation, the time between Jesus' first coming and His second. The Bible refers to this as the *Last days.*

[1]God, after He spoke long ago to the fathers in the prophets in many portions and in many ways,[2]in these last days has spoken to us in His Son, whom He appointed heir of all things, through whom also He made the world. -Hebrews 1:1-2 (NASB)

And some of the wonderful benefits of living in the last days are:

[17]'AND IT SHALL BE IN THE LAST DAYS,' says God,

'THAT I WILL POUR OUT MY SPIRIT UPON ALL MANKIND;

AND YOUR SONS AND YOUR DAUGHTERS SHALL PROPHESY,

AND YOUR YOUNG MEN SHALL SEE [divinely prompted] VISIONS,

AND YOUR OLD MEN SHALL DREAM [divinely prompted] DREAMS;

[18] EVEN ON MY BOND-SERVANTS, BOTH MEN AND WOMEN, I WILL IN THOSE DAYS POUR OUT MY SPIRIT

And they shall prophesy. -Acts 2:17-18 (AMP)

Peter is referencing the Prophet Joel - (Joel 2:28-29)

The Father sent the Holy Spirit on the day of Pentecost and He shares these revelatory expressions with Christians to experience, enjoy, and serve Him and others more effectively in these *Last Days*.

When we read our Bible and it says that something is true, we know it is true. There is an old saying that is appropriate here: "The Bible says it, I believe it, and that settles it." Always stick with the Bible. Do not let intellect (Mine, yours, or anyone else's) derail your life.

[18] For I assure you and most solemnly say to you, until heaven and earth pass away, not the smallest letter or stroke [of the pen] will pass from the Law until all things [which it foreshadows] are accomplished.
-Matthew 5:18 (AMP)

[4] But Jesus replied, "It is written and forever remains written, 'Man shall not live by bread alone, but by every word that comes out of the mouth of God.'" -
Matthew 4:4(AMP)

The reason why we started with this topic is so that each one of us can know that according to the Bible itself we live in the last days. So when you see signs, wonders, miracles, prophecy, healings, dreams and visions spoken of in the Bible, guess what? It is for you and me today! Very Exciting!

So be confident that according to the Bible itself, it is His will for His children to prophesy. Thanks be to our God who has fully equipped each believer for every good work! (See 2 Tim 3:16-17 & Heb. 13:20-21) We are privileged to have been hand selected by our God to live in these *Last Days*.

New Testament Prophecy

Old Testament Prophecy *in Contrast to* New Testament Prophecy

Let's begin with scripture that gives us a picture of this *contrast.*

[51] *Now when the time was approaching for Him to be taken up [to heaven], He was determined to go to Jerusalem [to fulfill His purpose].* [52] *He sent messengers on ahead of Him, and they went into a Samaritan village to make arrangements for Him;* [53] *but the people would not welcome Him, because He was traveling toward Jerusalem.* [54] *When His disciples James and John saw this, they said, "Lord, do You want us to command fire to come down from heaven and destroy them?"* [55] *But He turned and rebuked them [and He said, "You do not know what kind of spirit you are;* [56] *for the Son of Man did not come to destroy men's lives, but to save them."] And they journeyed on to another village. -Luke 9:51-56(AMP)*

To many, Elijah represents the prime example of an Old Testament prophet. As we see here, the disciples were still learning who Jesus really was and who they were in Him. They were not yet grasping why Jesus had come. They were still seeing through the eyes of Old Testament prophecy. So they wanted to pronounce judgement and destroy the people in the village just as Elijah had called down fire upon 100 soldiers and burned them up in 2 Kings 1:9-12. In the Old Testament people lived under the law: pretty much a lifestyle of *do and live according to the law and you will be blessed, or do your own thing and you will be cursed.* This reflects much of the Prophetic expression shared during that time period. New Testament prophecy is grace filled, love governed, and always Christ centered.

Let's look at what our New Testament guideline for prophecy is:

³ But [on the other hand] the one who prophesies speaks to people for edification [to promote their spiritual growth] and [speaks words of] encouragement [to uphold and advise them concerning the matters of God] and [speaks words of] consolation [to compassionately comfort them].
-1 Corinthians 14:3(AMP)

In this verse we see that prophecy must do these things:

* To build up and promote spiritual growth
* To encourage and call people near to Jesus
* To comfort with a greater degree of tenderness

Considering Luke 9:55 again, when Jesus said to the disciples "You don't know what kind of spirit you are." The disciples were still learning that Jesus had ushered in a new era for mankind, and with this new era all Christians are indwelt by God's precious Holy Spirit.

¹⁷ But the one who is united and joined to the Lord is one spirit with Him.
-I Corinthians 6:17 (AMP)

¹⁹ Do you not know that your body is a temple of the Holy Spirit who is within you, whom you have [received as a gift] from God, and that you are not your own [property]? ²⁰ You were bought with a price [you were actually purchased with the precious blood of Jesus and made His own]. So then, honor and glorify God with your body.
-I Corinthians 6:19-20 (AMP)

Now let's look deeper into the significance of being one spirit with Christ. His Spirit in us changes our relationship with God, relationships with other people and even our prophetic expression.

¹Beloved, do not believe every spirit [speaking through a self-proclaimed prophet]; instead, test the spirits to see whether they are from God, because many false prophets and teachers have gone out into the world. ² By this you know and recognize the Spirit of God: every spirit that acknowledges and confesses [the fact] that Jesus Christ has [actually] come in the flesh [as a man] is from God [God is its source];³ and every spirit that does not confess Jesus [acknowledging that He has come in the flesh, but would deny any of the Son's true nature] is not of God; this is the spirit of the antichrist, which you have heard is coming, and is now already in the world.
-1 John 4:1-3 (AMP)

•   In these verses in I John, why does Jesus coming in the flesh determine whether people can prophesy the right way or not? If a person has not trusted Jesus as Lord (being indwelled with the spirit of Jesus at salvation) it is impossible for their heart to be right with God, and right towards people.

•   Only when the Holy Spirit lives in us can we hear The Shepherds voice and prophesy with love and accuracy.

For the testimony of Jesus is the spirit of prophecy [His life and teaching are the heart of prophecy]."
-Revelation 19:10b (AMP)

New Testament prophecy is based on Jesus' testimony.

What was Jesus' testimony? What did Jesus say? What did Jesus do?

Jesus spoke to the people about the kingdom of God through teaching, demonstrating and explaining the scripture. He also unconditionally loved people and reconciled all who trusted in Him to Father God. Through a multitude of means, He connected people to their loving God. This is the Spirit of Prophecy. He has also entrusted us *Christians* with His ministry of reconciliation.

[18] But all these things are from God, who reconciled us to Himself through Christ [making us acceptable to Him] and gave us the ministry of reconciliation [so that by our example we might bring others to Him], [19] that is, that God was in Christ reconciling the world to Himself, not counting people's sins against them [but canceling them]. And He has committed to us the message of reconciliation [that is, restoration to favor with God][20] So we are ambassadors for Christ, as though God were making His appeal through us; we [as Christ's representatives] plead with you on behalf of Christ to be reconciled to God.
-2 Corinthians 5:18-20 (AMP)

Prophecy connects people to Jesus in a very unique way. It is one of many expressions of Jesus Himself and as such, it is a valuable part of the ministry of reconciliation that has been committed to us.

In the story of the woman at the well, John 4:7-42, Jesus Prophesied to her in verse 18 a *word of knowledge* and her life and many others were permanently changed as they believed in Jesus.

Be ready to hear. Be ready to share.

Prophecy is expressed most often in the *Church* or *Christian group* setting. I think this is because the church setting is where most Christians believe it should be expressed. The truth is that prophecy is for both the church and the world. So train yourself to continuously listen for the Holy Spirit's voice no matter where you are or who you are with.

Some of the ways God communicates to us are through the written word, the *Bible*, our prayer time and prophetic words from others. He will also use other forms of revelation. Each one of us must hear from God often for our relationship with Him to stay strong. Hearing His voice is crucial for our growth and development as Christians. Having regular input from God helps us to stay accurately on our course. God is most creative, and as such will speak to us through any means He chooses. He will also change some of His *means* of speaking to us from time to time. I believe this is a normal dynamic of any long-term growing relationship.

Vision and Calling

I believe that the terms vision and calling can be, and often are used interchangeably. Here is my effort to try and bring a little more distinction to each:

Calling

God's all-inclusive, life plan for an individual to be expressed over the course of their life.

Vision

Segmented views of God's life plan. This contains portions of our call that are given to us as we need them along the way.

The importance of vision is clearly seen in this verse:

Where there is no vision [no revelation of God and His word], the people are unrestrained; But happy and blessed is he who keeps the law [of God].
-Proverbs 29:18 (AMP)

Vision in this verse means something seen, a dream, revelation or Prophetic revelation. To be unrestrained means to not be lead, to wander around with uncertainty, no clear goals or boundaries.

Many years ago I heard Proverbs 29:18 explained like this: Where there is no ongoing, progressive revelation from God, the people wander around aimlessly until they die.

Sobering thought!

Several years ago I was preparing a teaching on prophecy for a church group. As I prayed, The Lord showed me a large funnel just like you would use to pour oil into your car only it was much larger. When I saw the image in my mind I said, "Lord what's this?" He then added to the image and I saw people in the funnel (the large entrance, opening). I saw the people very slowly moving deeper into the funnel, sometimes going forward, sometimes sideways or at an angle, some were even going around and around the inside of the large opening. Then I saw some of the people move into the narrow "neck" of the funnel and move much faster, more accurately through the rest of the funnel.

As I looked, I heard The Lord say, "Prophecy is like this funnel and when a person receives and responds to a prophetic word they move into the narrow neck of a funnel and their life accelerates more precisely on their God given course."

The Basics of Prophecy

When we trust Jesus as our Lord, the Holy Spirit comes and lives in us. At that moment we become part of God's family.

*[13] In Him, you also, when you heard the word of truth, the good news of your salvation, and [as a result] believed in Him, were stamped with the seal of the promised Holy Spirit [the One promised by Christ] as owned and protected [by God]. [14] The Spirit is the [a]guarantee [the first installment, the pledge, a foretaste] of our inheritance until the redemption of God's own [purchased] possession [His believers], to the praise of His glory.
-Ephesians 1:13-14 (AMP)*

This new family relationship has many benefits. One of which is that Jesus speaks to each of us regularly.

*[2] But he who enters by the door is the shepherd of the sheep [the protector and provider]. [3] The [a]doorkeeper opens [the gate] for this man, and the sheep hear his voice and pay attention to it. And [knowing that they listen] he calls his own sheep by name and leads them out [to pasture]. [4] When he has brought all his own sheep outside, he walks on ahead of them, and the sheep follow him because they know his voice and recognize his call.
-John 10:2-4 (AMP)*

*[16] I have other sheep [beside these] that are not of this fold. I must bring those also, and they will listen to My voice and pay attention to My call, and they will become one flock with one Shepherd.
-John 10:16(AMP)*

*[27] The sheep that are My own hear My voice and listen to Me; I know them, and they follow Me.
-John 10:27(AMP)*

Since Jesus is speaking to all of God's children often, why do so many Christians say that they are not hearing His voice? It is because God normally communicates differently than we are familiar with, so we must learn to recognize His voice. And once we learn to recognize His voice for

ourselves, we can hear God speak to us for others. This is called
"Prophecy." Prophecy is hearing from God and then sharing what you hear
with someone else.

* For [in this way] you can all prophesy one by one, so that everyone may
be instructed and everyone may be encouraged;
-I Corinthians 14:31 (AMP)*

Let's look at the four forms of revelation which comprise the prophetic
expression:

*⁸ For to one is given the word of wisdom through the Spirit, and to another
the word of knowledge according to the same Spirit; ⁹ to another faith by the
same Spirit, and to another gifts of healing by the one Spirit, ¹⁰ and to
another the effecting of miracles, and to another prophecy, and to another
the distinguishing of spirits, to another various kinds of tongues, and to
another the interpretation of tongues. -1 Corinthians 12:8-10(NASB)*

According to these verses they are:

* Word of Knowledge

* Word of Wisdom

* Discerning of Spirits

* Prophecy

Word of Knowledge

God sharing knowledge (facts or information) about someone's life. This can be a statement, event, place, object, image/picture, or people. This is specific in nature.

Word of Wisdom

This is different from a word of knowledge in that it is often God's perspective on something in our life. It can show what God is doing, what His will is, what His plan is, or what He desires for us in areas of our life. A word of wisdom contains needed information that helps us make wise decisions.

Often times a word of wisdom has a directional nature in it. Directional nature, meaning, that when we see where and what God is working on, confusion and divided focus disappear. And so, we are able to invest our life, time and resources more specifically into where God is for us as was revealed by the prophetic word of wisdom.

I cannot count how many times I have received a word of wisdom that spoke clearly into an area of my life that I was unsure of exactly what was going on, and *the fog lifted*. There was that *Aha!* Moment, *sometimes several*, as I saw God right there lovingly at work in that place in my life. And He and I connected right where I needed Him as a result of the prophetic word.

Discerning of Spirits

Discerning of Spirits means to distinguish between or judging between spirits. This can mean the Holy Spirit, things of the human spirit or soul. It can also be to distinguish between health, sickness, and disease. The natural world, fleshly things, angels, demons, Christ- given anointing's or calls upon people's lives, mantles, or gifts. While discerning of spirits is informational in nature it is more than that: it is more of a sensing or *knowing* in your spirit of the *origin* of something. When you discern something, it is like the information you received is quickly divided so you can help people in just the right place in their life. I believe this verse best describes my experience with discerning of spirits. This verse is speaking of the bigger scope of God's word, but the dividing nature of discerning of spirits is also captured in in this verse.

[12] *For the word of God is living and active and full of power [making it operative, energizing, and effective]. It is sharper than any two-edged sword, penetrating as far as the division of the soul and spirit [the completeness of a person], and of both joints and marrow [the deepest parts of our nature], exposing and judging the very thoughts and intentions of the heart. -Hebrews 4:12 (AMP)*

In my life, discerning of spirits functions like a doorway. God will often birth a prophetic word in me through that initial discernment moment. I will perceive something and as I give the thought or image my attention, a prophetic word will begin forming out of that initial discernment.

Of the four expressions of prophecy, discerning of spirits is the least understood. In my early years as a Christian, I remember being told that it was an ability to sense the devil or demonic activity in a situation or individual's life. While this is an aspect of this gift, the scope of it is much larger. The longer that my wife and I walk with God, the more we both enjoy (and rely on) the benefits of this gift. It is my belief that there are many Christians with the gift of discerning of spirits. I also believe that every person is born with a measure of Discerning of Spirits. This is another example of God's kindness to humanity. With this innate discerning from God, people are able to distinguish right from wrong and dangerous people from kind natured people. How many times have you heard someone say, "I have a gut feeling," or "Something feels wrong about this plan or that person?" This perception of good or bad, right or wrong, danger or safety have, I believe, their origin in discernment. While anyone can have a measure of this, Christians are blessed with a heightened spiritual awareness.

God gives some the *gift of discernment* which is an even greater level of discernment. And as with any God given gift or ability, we need it for ourselves and to help others. With discerning of spirits God can give a *divine knowing* that cuts through our thoughts or perceptions; helping us individually and also helping us to connect others with God at just the right spot in their life. In the life of a Christian, discerning can greatly expand and deepen. Over time, with the Holy Spirit and mentorship from seasoned Christians, this asset can greatly strengthen us and others.

Today's society tells us to accept everyone and ignore our perceptions concerning others. Because, after all, everyone is *really ok.* However, the more you ignore your internal *discerning/sensing*, the duller this asset becomes.

As Christians it is perfectly normal and right for us to act like Christians. I cannot tell you how many times my wife or I have had an impression about someone and then had this internal knowing/sensing confirmed. The way to cultivate discerning is by listening to it; not ignoring or pushing it aside. When we sense or feel something connected with a person, plan or activity. We should ask the Holy Spirit questions like, "What am I sensing? What are you showing me?"

As Christians it is perfectly normal and right for us to act like Christians

This *internal radar* if you will, can often be connected to an emotion or a feeling. There will be distinguishing characteristics to what we are sensing in our spirit. Over time, and with experience, a kind of *discerning data base* can be built. This data base is not a rigid system of interpreting what we are sensing, but more of a means to zero in; a starting point, so to speak. With the information we discerned at that moment, we cross-reference with previous similar experiences of discernment that were confirmed through interaction, conversation or ministry. We then can begin a dialogue with the Holy Spirit and through His leading we can more effectively, more precisely connect with others and help them connect with God. We need to continually refine *what these impressions mean.* As with any other gift or ability, the more we lovingly develop and use discerning of spirits, the more proficient we become.

Wait just a minute don't I know you?

I believe that most of us have had times in our life when we met someone for the first time and they reminded us of someone that we know, or knew in the past. The person will *seem or feel* exactly like or very close to the same as the other person we know or knew. This experience is not that uncommon. This strong impression that connects the two *personalities* in our mind, *sensing a clear similarity in these two people*, is very helpful to us as this information can be integrated into our interactions with them. If a person's presence, voice, fragrance (perfume, cologne), hair color/style etc. triggers strong memories of someone else, these impressions can also be from discerning of spirits. If you have this sense about someone, ask the Lord, "What is the connection that I am seeing between these two people and what do I do with it?"

Example:

Several years ago my wife introduced me to another man that a close friend of hers had just begun dating. As we approached him, before I had spoken to him, I looked at him and he reminded me very strongly of a man my mother had been married to. In that instant I clearly remembered all of the negative things that this man did to my mother and our family. These memories just flooded through my mind all at once. I knew that the Holy Spirit was showing me this person's *character*. As I prayerfully considered the impressions, I knew that this man's character was the same or very similar to the man my mother had been married to. After that initial meeting my wife asked me what I thought of him. I replied that the man would mistreat her friend, be abusive (emotionally and physically), and that he would not be faithful. My wife was a little surprised, but not a lot as these moments of discernment had happened to her and I before. We were unable to share these impressions with her friend, as the impression could have been wrong and hurtful. My wife's friend and the man were married. Several months later she contacted my wife, and said that she had broken off relationship with the man because he was abusive and unfaithful to their relationship.

Example Number Two:

I recently met a man and upon shaking his hand I felt, *discerned,* an overwhelming sense of my brother; this man felt like my brother. My brother's past and family dynamic as a child through young adulthood was quite unique. And through these unique experiences God produced a man who is loyal, dependable and fair with others. He is very much the *glue* of the family; keeping everyone connected. As I learned more about this man (that felt like my brother), I found out that his background was similar to my brother's. The man also possesses many of the same strengths and qualities that my brother has.

First Contact: We may discern information about someone or something at any time, but for me it happens most often and more consistently at first contact. That moment of first eye contact or that first handshake, Or when placing my hand on someone's shoulder to pray for them or the first few words of our conversation. Or it can occur that moment that I first enter a new area; building, town or other location, or touch an object. Be very aware of what you sense in those moments of first contact as God may give you needed information that will be helpful to yourself, or helpful for future interactions with people.

Prophecy

While *prophecy* includes all of these other three expressions, the word prophecy itself means foretelling future events. Often this *foretelling* will connect with and reinforce what God is and has been doing in a person's life already. It can be like seeing the next step or steps that are in the future.

Timing in Prophecy

When we receive revelation and sense that something will happen *soon* or *within a certain timeframe*, we need to be careful to not communicate an exact time that it will happen in the future. I and others have learned that accurately knowing timing in revelation can be very difficult. There are occasions where God will plainly state a time or date, but this is not the norm. Even if you or I have a sense of *general* timing (soon, months, years, etc.) it is normally good to leave this information out of the prophecy when shared. I have witnessed prophecies given to people over the years that had specific timelines in them and these timelines proved to be unhelpful to the recipient as they can produce an unhealthy expectation on God, themselves, and others around them.

How God Speaks

Now that we have looked at the four expressions of prophecy, we need to look at how God speaks to us. The Bible lists many ways that God speaks with His children. God is creative in His nature, and as such He is creative in how He communicates with His children. Here are *some* of the ways He communicates with us.

Partial List

Dreams, visions, images (pictures) in our minds, internal small still *gentle* voice, external audible voice, our emotions, riddles, puzzles, impressions or physical feelings in our bodies, questions and left field thoughts.

Dreams: Everyone dreams from time to time. Some dreams are not important, but may be prompted by any number of things in our life. However, if you have a dream that you believe is significant and you think the Lord may be trying to speak with you through it, write it down and begin to pray and ask God questions about it. Ask God to reveal the dream's meaning. If you believe God has spoken to you or given you a message for someone else, see if the message lines up with scripture and the counsel of others.

Visions: This is a waking dream, so to speak. Sometimes this could be like a daydream (where you are totally in control) or it could be more overwhelming (where you are not in control but more of a spectator as it unfolds in your mind). Both of these can be from God.

Images in our minds: A picture that you would not have thought of just pops into your mind as you are going about your daily life.

Riddles/Puzzles: You receive a partial image, impression, or dream. It does not communicate clearly but peaks your interest. Pray and ask God who this is for and how it connects. Look up the meaning of what you received in the dictionary, Bible and other resources. Ask God to connect the dots. This can feel very much like a hunt that involves prayer and study. The Bible has several examples of Riddles and Dark sayings. Things can remain unknown unless they are sought out through prayer and study:

For further examples see:

Then a shoot will spring from the spring of Jesse and a branch will bear fruit. -Isaiah 11:1

This is speaking of Jesus but you would not know it if that is all the Lord initially showed you unless you researched, sought out or hunted its meaning.

Luke 8:17, Daniel 2:47, Proverbs 25:2

Impressions: A strong emotion when you are around someone or something and you can't explain why. This could be intense empathy, remorse, sadness, grief, joy, accomplishment, or happiness. You could be sensing God's heart for yourself, or you could be picking up on the state of another person's heart. It could be having a song come to mind and you can't get it out of your head. Ask God if there is more to it than a catchy tune. Maybe God is trying to encourage you or if someone comes to mind, this could be prompting you to encourage them or pray for them.

Physical senses in our bodies, smells, tastes, hearing: This is a physical sensation. It could be a pain in your body that is not normally there. It may be that someone near to you (in your presence) or someone not in your presence needs healing and God is prompting you to pray for that part of their body. It could be a smell that triggers a memory for no apparent reason. A certain taste that reminds you of someone such as mom's lasagna or a memory of food you ate with a friend. Any physical sensation that interrupts your day and brings your thoughts to a person, situation or event could be a God led moment where He desires you to pray or speak encouragement to someone.

Left field thoughts: You could have what you feel is a distracting thought about another person or situation you are involved in. Your attention could be on your work or a project you are completing and then out of nowhere, you are drawn in thought to a person or group or situation. God could be leading you there to hear from Him and gain His perspective.

As we pay attention to what we are sensing and respond in prayer and conversation with God, He may expound and give us encouragement for ourselves or others that will bring life, hope and peace where needed.

A life and Power of His own

While God does speak to us in many ways, there is one unique characteristic that helps us recognize His voice. However He speaks to us, His word has a life and power of its own (His own). There are no human words that can express this, but here's the closest I can say: God's word carries not only his thoughts, but His power, His nature, His expansive personality, His overwhelming love. I am not referring to the powerfulness, volume or loudness with which He communicates with us, but the uniqueness; His individuality that is His voice. A good example of this is how the ocean looks as we stand on the seashore. We see the water and the waves, but there is also an *undertow* that is not seen, but is felt as you stand or swim in the ocean. God's revelation is like this, there is what we see or hear, but as we start asking God questions and *get into it* there is His undertow of Himself there. His power contained in His word is not always huge or overwhelming it is just very unique, very Himself. I hope my weak attempt here to define God's voice in words will help in recognizing when He is speaking to you.

Some Helpful Contrast

To help make this clearer, when a thought originates with us, the thought is only as strong as we make and keep it. Our human nature powers our thoughts. As soon as we place our attention on something else, our previous thoughts weaken. They lose their potency and strength. Our thoughts require our energy/strength and attention to keep them alive and strong. The following is a negative example of the process of feeding thoughts:

[13] *Let no man say when he is tempted, "I am tempted by God," for God can't be tempted by evil, and he himself tempts no one.* [14] *But each one is tempted when he is drawn away by his own lust, and enticed.* [15] *Then the lust, when it has conceived, bears sin; and the sin, when it is full grown, produces death. -James 1:13-15 (WEB)*

This same process is true with the devil or his demons. He may give us a thought, but his thoughts, *fiery darts* -Eph. 6:16, or any human thoughts quickly lose their strength if we do not keep them alive. Peter gives us a great example of our *limited* power and God's *unlimited* power.

[24] *For, "All flesh is like grass, And all its glory like the flower of grass. The grass withers, And the flower falls off,* [25] *But the word of the Lord endures forever. -1 Peter 1:24-25a NASB*

Even if God drops a *good idea* into your mind, it will be different than any other thought that originated in you or elsewhere.

• A God word or thought has within it all the power needed to sustain it until fulfillment

• For the word of God is living and powerful

[12] For the word of God is living and active and full of power [making it operative, energizing, and effective]. -Hebrews 4:12a (AMP)

• It shall not return void

So will My word be which goes out of My mouth; It will not return to Me void (useless, without result), Without accomplishing what I desire, And without succeeding in the matter for which I sent it. -Isaiah 55:11 (AMP)

• God's word stands forever

The grass withers, the flower fades, But the word of our God stands forever. -Isaiah 40:8 (AMP)

• The word of God lives and abides forever

[23] for you have been born again [that is, reborn from above—spiritually transformed, renewed, and set apart for His purpose] not of seed which is perishable but [from that which is] imperishable and immortal, that is, through the living and everlasting word of God.
-I Peter 1:23 (AMP)

When God speaks to us, His word has His power, His strength, His nature, and His purity are in it. You can look at it, scrutinize it, pray about it, give it a few days, and then look at it again. It will be just as powerful and fresh as when He first spoke it to you. I also believe that God in His kindness provides this *staying power* of His spoken word to give us adequate time to pray about the word, seek wise counsel, and receive confirmation from others we trust and then make good decisions.

Interpreting Revelation

When we believe that God has spoken to us, this could be by an image or picture, soft internal voice, movie clip, impressions in our minds or our bodies, what then? How should we respond? Often when God speaks to us it requires some investigation, a deliberate Q and A with the Holy Spirit; a sorting out or *sifting*. I believe there is a God created response built into each person. A divine curiosity in us that is stimulated by His word, written or spoken. When God speaks to us, this *curiosity* is lovingly aroused causing us to want to draw near to God and receive what He has for us. If we do not respond to God's word with a humble curiosity, we can miss what He wants to share with us.

Here is a beautiful example:

¹Now Moses was keeping the flock of Jethro (Reuel) his father-in-law, the priest of Midian; and he led his flock to the west side of the wilderness and came to Horeb (Sinai), the mountain of God. ²The[a]Angel of the LORD appeared to him in a blazing flame of fire from the midst of a bush; and he looked, and behold, the bush was on fire, yet it was not consumed. ³ So Moses said, "I must turn away [from the flock] and see this great sight—why the bush is not burned up."⁴ When the LORD saw that he turned away [from the flock] to look, God called to him from the midst of the bush and said, "Moses, Moses!" And he said, "Here I am." -Exodus 3:1-4 (AMP)

In these verses we see Moses choose to stop what he was doing and *turn away.* Curiosity had gripped him, and then he investigated why the bush didn't burn up. In verse four when the Lord saw that Moses stopped what he was doing and gave this special event his full attention, God spoke to him. This God stirred curiosity expressed through giving God our full attention looks a lot like this:

[2] Make your ear attentive to wisdom,
Incline your heart to understanding;
[3] For if you cry for discernment,
Lift your voice for understanding;
[4] If you seek her as silver
And search for her as for hidden treasures;
[5] Then you will discern the fear of the Lord
And discover the knowledge of God.
-Proverbs 2:2-5(NASB)

The next quality needed to interpret revelation is a humble attitude. In Genesis 40:8, Pharaoh's Butler and Baker were in prison with Joseph and they each had a dream. They spoke to Joseph and said to him that no one could interpret their dreams. Joseph responds, "Do not interpretations belong to God?" And then in Genesis 41:1-36, Pharaoh has two dreams and calls for Joseph. In verse 15, Pharaoh says to Joseph "You can understand and interpret dreams," and Joseph says in verse 16 "It is not in me. God will give Pharaoh a favorable answer." God used Joseph greatly because Joseph knew himself and his God. Another great example is found in Daniel chapter two. King Nebuchadnezzar had dreams and Daniel speaks to the King in verse 28 and 29 saying, there is a God in heaven that reveals secrets, and in verse 30 Daniel says, I am nothing special.

We can see Joseph and Daniel's humility. Humility is, I believe, the greatest of virtues. We need it in ever increasing amounts to receive from God as well as to minister to people. We should aspire to have the same attitude that John the Baptist had.

[30] *He must increase [in prominence], but I must decrease. -John 3:30(AMP)*

And two more verses that speak of humility are:

[24] *Then Jesus said to His disciples, "If anyone wishes to come after Me, he must deny himself, and take up his cross and follow Me.* [25] *For whoever wishes to save his life will lose it; but whoever loses his life for My sake will find it. -Matthew 16:24-25(NASB)*

The treasure hunt is on!

When God shares revelation/prophecy with us, it is often very much like an amazing time of hide and seek between us and our loving father! Parents remember those wonderful times of hide and seek with your children? I remember that the highlight of the experience was being found! I believe this is exactly how Father God feels. He loves spending time with us so much that He hides things just well enough for us to seek Him so our relationship and our love for one another will increase! Oh, and guess what? He loves being found just like we parents do by our children!

Have a look at this beautiful scripture:

[7] *"Ask and keep on asking and it will be given to you; seek and keep on seeking and you will find; knock and keep on knocking and the door will be opened to you.* [8] *For everyone who keeps on asking receives, and he who keeps on seeking finds, and to him who keeps on knocking, it will be opened.* -Matthew 7:7-8 (AMP)*

This scripture applies in any area of our lives, and also accurately describes the process of interpreting revelation. Now let's spend some time looking at a few helpful things to be aware of while interpreting.

As you look at what God showed you or think about what He said, pay close attention to it. Is anything changing, or expanding, is there a part of the revelation being emphasized? Is there something that seems to *stand out* or be *highlighted* in a sense? What about the setting? Any colors or sounds? What about numbers i.e. three flowers, two trees etc.? Do you feel emotionally stirred? If so, in what way?

I am referring to the emotions felt in the revelation. While the revelation is being received, or while examining the revelation and interpreting it, these emotions can be a vital part of the revelation and *may* be a necessary part of the interpretation and expression of the prophetic word. However, please keep in mind that our emotions can be unpredictable and as such they *may* play no relevant part in interpreting revelation. This may seem vague and indecisive, but there is no clear *black and white* way to say that any emotion is always a God given part of a revelation.

Some helpful tips on emotions sensed or felt in connection with received revelation are: Does the emotion fit or bring clarity to a part of or to the whole revelation? Does the emotion help in expressing God's heart to the other person? Does the emotion release the fruit of the spirit through the sharing of the prophetic word? Did the emotion seem to come out of left field or nowhere? Does the emotion seem to rise up in the revelation like a gentle, or even a strong breeze? Much like when we are standing outside gazing at a beautiful setting on a warm summer's day. The view is great and we are happy to see it, and then all of a sudden a cool breeze blows and makes the setting complete. That is very much how a God given emotion happens in a revelation. It just takes something perfect and makes it better or complete. Emotions are very important for us to pay attention to as God gave them to us, and He himself is very emotional. *He jealously loves.* In fact, His name is Jealous (Exodus 34:14). His joy is our strength (Nehemiah 8:10). Here are a few other verses that speak of the positive value of emotions: Mt 9:36 & 20:34, Luke 10:33-34 &15:20 & 19:41-42, Acts 17:16-17, Heb. 13:3, 1Peter 3:8.

Sometimes God will use our emotions to express His heart through us. Have a look at the 9 fruits of the Spirit, see (Galatians 5:22-23). There is quite an emotional element contained in their expression! In fact, the Bible says that love is greater than any gift or other expression. True, fervent, passionate love is very emotional!

Connecting the Pieces

As these components become clearer and things begin to fit together, keep in mind the big picture as well as all of the details. The big picture of revelation is the *scope,* or the full setting, the overall theme of the revelation. Everything fits within this big picture.

Details are important, but the details normally fit into, and are part of the bigger picture. Just like scripture must be interpreted in context; so should our prophetic interpretations be. I am sure that by now you can see that there is a lot to accurately interpreting revelation. But God is faithful, and will give us everything we need to follow Him and help others. So please be patient with yourself, enjoy God, and be patient with yourself, *I meant to say that twice.*

Learning to rest in God while interpreting revelation is important. Interpretation cannot be forced or rushed. I have found that in patiently considering what God has shared with me, observing it, doing some research when necessary and prayerfully asking questions, the Holy Spirit will show me what He wanted me to know.

When God gives the revelation; He will also give the interpretation. He is faithful! We must learn to be *restfully pro-active* while interpreting revelation.

On occasion we may receive a word of knowledge, *a fact,* and as we consider this specific information, it does not change. Does not expand, or have more information added to it. It just stays the same, solid and clear. When this happens, view this as the complete revelation, and share exactly what you received. Let's look at a few tools that help with interpretation.

#1- The Bible. The written word is the number one tool for interpreting revelation from God. See 2 Timothy 3:16-17. Also, in 2 Peter 1:19 it says that we have a "More sure word of prophecy." The Bible is absolutely sure and perfectly solid. It is the standard by which all prophecy is to be judged. Any prophetic revelation we receive that disagrees with the written word is to be viewed as inaccurate.

The Bible is also the best source for doing research to interpret the revelation we receive. If you see symbols or objects in the revelation, see if they are in Scripture. What is their meaning in the Bible? Was there a scripture reference in the revelation? Look it up. This brings up something else: Our need to spend much time reading and studying our Bibles. The better you and I know God's written word, the better we will know the living word (Jesus), and the quicker and easier it will be for us to hear and understand His spoken word.

> The better you and I know God's written word, the better we will know the Living Word, Jesus, and the quicker and easier it will be for us to hear and understand His spoken word

If the revelation contains objects, pictures, tools, vehicles etc., prayerfully look online and see what are the normal or common uses for these things. What, if any, are the special *characteristics* mentioned in your research of the object or picture you saw/heard in the revelation? Is the thing *common* or *rare*? The process of interpreting is another great part of our God adventure!

Another very helpful resource is: "The Ultimate Guide to Understanding the Dreams you Dream," by Ira Milligan. While this book focuses on dreams, I have found it very good resource for interpreting other types of prophetic revelation as well.

For about twenty five plus years, every so often I will smell a strange smoldering smell as if there is a wire shorting out and burning through the insulation (plastic covering) on it. That combined with some kind of incense. No one else has ever been able to smell it with me. For many years I could not figure out what this was until I prayed and specifically asked God what it was. He showed me that each time that I smelled it He was doing a significant work in my life and a part of me, *my selfishness,* was dying or *being sacrificed.* Going up in smoke as incense. I immediately said to God *jokingly,* "So that is my butt that is smoldering, Huh?" Now when I smell it, He and I laugh together, and I thank Him for His faithfulness to complete what He started in me.

Clock Example

I went through a period of about four months where I could not go to sleep until one am. Or when I fell asleep, I would wake up and look at the clock and it would be one a.m. This went on day after day, until finally I decided to ask God what was going on. I felt that He wanted me to do some research. I did and discovered that the number one meant *new beginnings.* I thanked Him as this affirmed other things He had been saying to me, and in about one year, my wife and I experienced a huge *new beginning* in our lives! This was the first time that God had used the clock to speak to me.

Words of Warning

There are times when God will give a warning to be shared with an individual or group. Warnings happen much less often than other types of prophecy, but on occasion they do. Warnings are a *call to action* as they have a powerful sense of urgency in them. These words are clear and concise so that the recipient can make a good decision promptly. One thing that needs to be said here is that the goal of a word of warning is not to produce fear. It will have at its heart an urgency to make God focused changes where necessary. To wholeheartedly connect with God, respond appropriately; enlist His power, His plans, and His resources into our now. I would like to share two examples of words of warning.

Example 1

Many years ago my sister-in-law was dating a man who had a violent and unstable personality. This man did not like my mother-in-law. As I was in prayer one day, God warned me that this man was planning to harm my mother-in-law.

The warning was urgent and quite powerful. I promptly shared this with my wife, mother-in-law, and a few others to pray. We diligently prayed and sought God for protection from this man. My sister-in-law asked the man about it, and he confirmed that he was planning to harm my mother-in-law "soon." Three days later as he and his cousin were on the way to the house planning to harm her, there was an accident that completely removed them from our family. Their access was denied. God intervened!

God warned us so we could pray and partner with Him for this dear lady's protection. I would like to add something here. She was a single mom raising her grandkids. While God watches out for and protects all his children, I believe He is particularly involved in the care and protection of single moms who trust in him, and fatherless children. See Psalms 10:14, 68:5, 82:3 &146:9.

Example 2

About 20 years ago in prayer the Lord showed me a picture of a man I barely knew. As I pondered the image I clearly heard, "pray for this man and his family's safety." I did immediately, but felt strongly that I needed to connect with him, physically lay hands on him, pray for him, and for his family's safety. I got in contact with him and shared what I felt like God wanted. He agreed, so I went to his home and prayed with him and his family. I placed my hand on his shoulder as I felt the Holy Spirit had instructed me to do and we prayed together.

I left and went home. He contacted me two days later and shared that the day after we had prayed together he and his family were involved in a bad car accident. The vehicle that he, his wife, and daughter were in had lost control and flipped multiple times, totaling and destroying the vehicle. He showed me pictures of the vehicle. Neither he, his wife, nor daughter were injured, not even a scratch! Praise be to our God!!! This testimony of God's protection impacted many in the area in the days that followed. Jesus got all the glory!

There are some common things I have seen in each word of warning I have received or heard of others receiving. Each one received was sharp and clear, much like a very potent word of knowledge. They are very strong, clear facts that require no interpretation. It's like this: here is the information you need, now do something with it! There is also an overwhelming sense of urgency. Every warning that I and others have received was *time sensitive* in nature. God was sharing absolutely necessary information right in time to change negative, possibly deadly, outcomes.

While these types of words are not that common, when they happen, our response must be prompt. We must immediately enter into prayer and seek God for confirmation in our spirit and make sure to share the word with the person it is for ASAP. Include leaders or others helpful to the person or group the word is for. If the word is for you and you believe the word is accurate, make whatever God led changes are necessary. Have others who you trust and that care about you cover you in prayer through this response time. Please do not take lightly a word of warning.

CHAPTER 2

Prophetic How-To

Moving in Opposites

Seeing Past the Obvious

Delivery Matching Content

Sharing Prophetic Words

Personal Responsibility

Moving in Opposites

We just looked at New Testament prophecy which builds others up, encourages them, strengthens their relationship with God and also tenderly comforts them. What do we do when we receive something that does not fit within these guidelines? Let's go a step farther, what if we receive something negative, perverted, or just plain bad? How do we responsibly steward, interpret, and share this kind of revelation?

Prophesying the Devil's plans

Years ago, there was a youth rally and a woman was praying over a young man. She shared with him that the Lord showed her he had a problem with pornography. She shared this information publicly in front of his friends and youth leader exposing and embarrassing him. Sharing this word did not produce any fruit in his life other than a bad impression of God and His children.

The truth is, from time to time God may show us negative things in the lives of others. When we receive this type of information, we must remember that whether the revelation is now truth, future potential truth, past truth or no truth at all, God's plans are always for our good. He sees the best in us and will not put us to shame.

So, why would God show us something like this? There is a good reason. Let's look at some scripture that will help us to lovingly interpret and share this type of revelation. The Bible says in Romans 10:11 (NASB) (also see roman 9:33b)

" For the Scripture says, "WHOEVER BELIEVES IN HIM WILL NOT BE DISAPPOINTED."(Lit put to shame)- Romans 10:11 (NASB)

When we receive negative revelation, we know without a doubt that it is not God's will or plan for a person. Also in 3 John vs. 2 (AMP) it says:

2 Beloved, I pray that in every way you may succeed and prosper and be in good health [physically], just as [I know] your soul prospers [spiritually].

Prosper here means an ongoing progress of state of success and well-being in every area of our lives. We also know that any revelation we share with the person must fit the biblical guidelines of 1 Corinthians 14:3. So here is how we handle this type of revelation:

We do it by *moving in opposites.* For a clear picture of this let's look at the Scripture.

The devil and Jesus

In John 10:10 (AMP) 10 The thief comes only in order to steal and kill and destroy. I came that they may have and enjoy life, and have it in abundance [to the full, till it overflows]. In John 8:44 & Revelation 20:10 the devil is a murderer, liar and deceiver. In Mark 4:15 he is the thief who steals. And in Matthew 4:1 he tempted/tested the Lord Jesus. He also does the same to us. In Revelation 12: 10 he is the accuser.

Now let's look at Jesus. Beginning at *1 John 3:8b (AMP) The Son of God appeared for this purpose, to destroy the works of the devil.* For contrast, let's look at some of the ways Jesus destroys the devils work. The devil steals – Jesus gave himself for us Galatians 1:4. The devil steals, kills and destroys – Jesus gives us abundant life John 10:10.

Here is a wonderful list of some of Jesus' benefits to us:

² Bless and affectionately praise the Lord, O my soul,
And do not forget any of His benefits;
³ Who forgives all your sins,
Who heals all your diseases;
⁴ Who redeems your life from the pit,
Who crowns you [lavishly] with
lovingkindness and tender mercy;
-Psalm 103:2-4 (AMP)

The devil is a liar. Jesus said, "I am the Way, the truth, and the life." - John 14:6. The devil is our opponent, he is against us – but Jesus is our friend. -Luke 12:4. The devil is a slanderer, falsely accusing us – Jesus is seated at the right hand of God interceding for us. He lives to make intercession for us. -Romans 8:34 & Hebrews 7:25. The devil is the accuser or deceiver – Jesus is our advocate/our representative -1 John 2:1. The devil is evil – Jesus is good -Psalms 136:1

I wanted to present a clear contrast of how opposite Jesus and the devil are. This biblical principle is the basis for moving in opposites. For every negative revelation that God has shown us, Jesus has an overwhelming life-changing positive!! As Jesus destroyed the works of the devil, so are we to keep on doing with our words and our deeds/actions.

The reason we sometimes see or hear negative things is so we can *move in opposites.* By doing this we can directly and specifically speak God's life and plans into areas that the person is struggling in, or into areas that the devil means to harm them. When the Lord shows us something negative, I believe it is to stir up and release not only prophetic revelation, but also a fierce love and care for the person. It is heartbreaking to see a person struggling in bondage, or to see the devils influence upon their lives. We should become angry and burn with the zeal of the Lord for them. Then this zeal mixes with, and saturates the prophetic word we share with them.

Here's a scripture that conveys this huge, expansive release of love.

11 For as high as the heavens are above the earth,
So great is His lovingkindness toward those who fear Him.
12 As far as the east is from the west,
So far has He removed our transgressions from us.

[13]Just as a father has compassion on his children,
So the LORD has compassion on those who fear Him.
-Psalms 103:11-13 (NASB)

Our God is so amazing!

In this scripture He shares in human words something that we cannot comprehend! When we read this we can't help but go, "Wow!" And wonder at the huge love that God has for us! It is the span between the heavens and the earth, and the east from the west. This huge span is not an empty void. It is a massive area of love filled, grace packed relationship and care. This giant amount of love and care saturates the prophetic word as it is shared. I hope this in some way touches on the truth of why God will show us negative things so we can more fully express His huge love for the person. This gap between the negative we see, *but don't share,* and the beautiful plan of God, *shared with the person,* destroys the negative works of the devil. The Bible says in Romans 12:21 (NASB), do not be overcome by evil, but overcome evil with good. That is exactly what we're doing whenever we *move in opposites.*

Here are some examples to consider

If we receive this	Prayerfully Consider Sharing
Fear	Love
Sorrow, Discouragement	Joy/ Gods pleasure
Turmoil/ Worry	Peace
Impatience/Anxiousness	Patience/Gods perfect timing
Unkindness/Hostility	Kindness/gentleness
A lack of integrity	Goodness /virtue/integrity

Continued

If we receive this	Prayerfully Consider Sharing
Unfaithfulness/Infidelity	Faithfulness/ Faith
Independence/ Unyieldedness	Meekness/Gentleness
Indulgence/Excess/Carelessness	Self-control/Temperance

We know that God desires Christians to have the fruit of the Spirit. See Galatians 5:22-23. The *Prayerfully consider sharing* column above demonstrates what moving in opposites would look like. For example, while praying with someone, you believe the Lord revealed to you that the other person struggles with being independent. I would share with the person that I believe the Lord has made them strong and He desires to partner with them by working meekness and gentleness into their life.

If we see turmoil or worry, we know God has peace and calmness for them. A desire for them to cast their cares upon the Lord (Ps.55:22, Phil.4:6-7 & 1Pet.5:7). This is a great opportunity for a prophetic word and scripture pairing. If we see perversion, we know God has a call to purity and uprightness on their lives. If we see a life long struggle, we know God wants them free and victorious.

These are just three examples but it gives you the picture.

If we receive something negative from the Lord, immediately start a conversation with the Holy Spirit. I do something like this: Dear Holy Spirit, you showed me this,"_____." What would you like me to say that will bring *your* heart, plans, and perfect will into this person's life to help them?

If you do not have a healthy, God honoring and person honoring way to share the word, the opposite of the negative information you received, don't share the word with them. And please don't tell the person that you received something from God, but can't share it. This will only stir their curiosity and make a very awkward conversation. If you are already ministering to them, pray with them and bless them. After the interaction, pray and talk with God about what you received. It may have been just for you to know how to more effectively pray for them or maybe the Holy Spirit will help you interpret it so it can be shared with them at a later time. If unsure, always stick with love and respect.

Seeing Past the Obvious

Here we will be discussing the importance of listening and looking to God, while at the same time ignoring or *blocking out* natural input. This can be difficult as we are learning to tune in to God and hear from Him for ourselves and others. To help illustrate this, think about yourself for a moment. We all experience times and seasons in which we have a lot of things happening. Our minds can be very busy dealing with sudden issues, stressful relationships, or family issues. Life happens to all of us, but as Christians we have the most interesting of lives, being citizens of two realms. We trusted Christ and right then at that moment became a citizen of the kingdom of God, see Colossians 1:12-13 & Ephesians 2:19. We also became joint heirs with Jesus -Romans 8:17. Praise God! But, we also live in the natural world. This double existence creates some unique and sometimes challenging thought processes within our minds. If that weren't enough, we also have eternal life, the moment we trusted Jesus and are each day being saved, sanctified. -1 Corinthian's 1:18, 1 Thess.4:3, 1 Cor.1:29-31 & Phil.2:12-13. This ongoing process in our lives of separating the natural man -fleshly desires i.e. *selfishness,* from the spiritual -God and others

centered/*selflessness*. All of this going on in one body can be quite
challenging.

In prophecy, as in our Christian life, there is a need to become
proficient at separating thoughts and information in our minds. Learning to
quickly connect with God and subject what is going on in our head to His
authority. Let's look at some Biblical examples of natural and spiritual or
God input. Let's go to the Bible and see a great example of the need for us
to be able to separate natural and spiritual input.

In Joshua Ch. 9:3-16, we see that the people of Gibeon crafted a plan
to deceive Joshua and the people of Israel. They showed the Israelites their
stuff, lied to them and convinced them to make a peace treaty, and Joshua
agreed. Verse 14 is the key: the Israelites made decisions based on natural
input and natural knowledge. They did not hold all of this knowledge out at
arm's length, and inquire of the Lord.

*[3] When the inhabitants of Gibeon heard what Joshua had done to Jericho
and to Ai, [4] they also acted craftily and set out as envoys, and took worn-out
sacks on their donkeys, and wineskins worn-out and torn and mended, [5]
and worn-out and patched sandals on their feet, and worn-out clothes on
themselves; and all the bread of their provision was dry and had become
crumbled. [6] They went to Joshua to the camp at Gilgal and said to him and
to the men of Israel, "We have come from a far country; now therefore,
make a covenant with us." [7] The men of Israel said to the Hivites, "Perhaps
you are living within our land; how then shall we make a covenant with
you?" [8] But they said to Joshua, "We are your servants." Then Joshua said
to them, "Who are you and where do you come from?" [9] They said to him,
"Your servants have come from a very far country because of the fame of
the Lord your God; for we have heard the report of Him and all that He
did in Egypt, [10] and all that He did to the two kings of the Amorites who*

were beyond the Jordan, to Sihon king of Heshbon and to Og king of Bashan who was at Ashtaroth. [11] So our elders and all the inhabitants of our country spoke to us, saying, 'Take provisions in your hand for the journey, and go to meet them and say to them, "We are your servants; now then, make a covenant with us."' [12] This our bread was warm when we took it for our provisions out of our houses on the day that we left to come to you; but now behold, it is dry and has become crumbled. [13] These wineskins which we filled were new, and behold, they are torn; and these, our clothes and our sandals are worn out because of the very long journey." [14] So the men of Israel took some of their provisions, and did not ask for the counsel of the Lord. [15] Joshua made peace with them and made a covenant with them, to let them live; and the leaders of the congregation swore an oath to them. [16] It came about at the end of three days after they had made a covenant with them, that they heard that they were neighbors and that they were living within their land. -Joshua 9:3-16 (NASB)

Let's look at another example of this as God sends Samuel to Jesse's house to anoint David as king of Israel:

[6] So it happened, when they had come, he looked at Eliab [the eldest son] and thought, "Surely the Lord's anointed is before Him." [7] But the Lord said to Samuel, "Do not look at his appearance or at the height of his stature, because I have rejected him. For the Lord sees not as man sees; for man looks [a]at the outward appearance, but the Lord looks at the heart." -1 Samuel 16:6-7 (AMP)

Keep God first in every area or interaction in our lives.

Isaiah says this beautifully:

Who is blind but My servant,
Or so deaf as My messenger whom I send?
Who is so blind as he that is at peace with Me,
Or so blind as the servant of the Lord?
-Isaiah 42:19(NASB)

- Blind and deaf to natural input.
- Single-minded to serve God, and to deliver his message.

While this disciplining of our mind can be difficult, especially at first, it is crucial to clearly hear from God and accurately deliver prophetic words. One last comment; these scriptures and the teaching here are not saying to be insensitive or uncaring toward others. But we need to develop a disciplined mind-set to listen for God first in our lives, ministries, and interactions so we can more effectively partner with Him.

Delivery Matching Content

When we believe God has given us a word, *prophetic revelation* for someone, the way in which we deliver the word is very important. A great deal can potentially be lost in the delivery of prophecy. While God's word will accomplish what it is sent forth to do, (See Isaiah 55:11), I do believe that we should do our very best to effectively convey Gods heart and his words. Several studies have shown that most of human communication is non-verbal; somewhere between 60 and 90%. This non-verbal communication is composed of body language, facial expressions, postures, hand gestures, etc. and the much smaller part of our communication being verbal between 10 and 40%. So with this in mind, we can be sure that there are times where God wants us to communicate his revelation, *prophecy*, through any of and sometimes several of these means of communication.

When it comes to delivering a word, let's look at some examples of delivery and content matching. If we share a word that God is giving the person boldness, we should speak boldly. Stand up straight, with confidence, conveying strength in posture and attitude, and make confident eye contact.

If the word speaks of God's peace and comfort, we should speak calmly, gently, and peacefully while having a posture of acceptance. A kind smile fits here as well. Holding the other person's hand could also reinforce the experience, if appropriate.

We can sometimes receive words that have many different elements, feelings, emotions and settings that we must endeavor to accurately share. Being open and eager to be used by God through any and all means available to us increases our effectiveness prophetically. Let's look at some Biblical examples of God speaking through people in many ways.

Please read

Isaiah 20:1-4

Jeremiah chapter 27

Ezekiel 4:1-8

Ezekiel chapter 12

Hosea beginning with chapter 1

Acts 21:10-11

An example of delivery matching content

A few years back there was a transition in the leadership of our church. The senior pastor transferred his position in the church to another man and as I prayed for the transition service, I asked God if He would like to share anything through me as I participated in this transition.

The Lord showed me that this was a passing of the baton to this next group of leaders. But, that He was giving a brand new baton to the leaving senior pastor and his wife for the next leg of their race, and that they would carry this baton until the end of their race here on earth.

I had a strong sense that the senior pastor who was leaving felt like he had handed off his baton to the next generation and was unsure of what was ahead for him in kingdom work. God gave me a powerful impression that He wanted this man and his wife to know *tangibly* that this was the beginning of the next leg, a *new* leg of their race. Not just a *handing off* of the baton and then off they go into an unknown future. As I considered this word, the tangible part gripped me, so I knew that I needed to tangibly communicate this word to them. So, I made a baton out of a very special hardwood. Wood that is known for its durability, longevity, and high oil content, *symbolizing the Holy Spirit in their life*. I felt that this tangible object would enhance the clarity of the prophecy.

As the transition happened, the new leadership and I gathered around the departing senior pastor and his wife. As I extended the baton to him and his wife's hands, the new leaders and I along with the departing senior pastor and his wife all held the baton together. As we held it, I shared the word, and then the new leaders and I released the baton into the departing pastor and his wife's hand. I enthusiastically said to him and his wife "Run!" This is a great example of how delivery and content matched.

I am not saying to turn every prophetic word into a drama or skit. That would be inappropriate. What I am communicating here is that when you receive a prophetic word be aware of how to communicate it most effectively. Taking into account the setting, and time constraints, if any, and the resources you have available. God created each of us with everything we need to clearly share his love with those around us.

[31] So then, whether you eat or drink or whatever you do, do all to the glory of [our great] God. -1 Corinthians 10:31 (AMP)

Sharing Prophetic Words

Every prophetic word has two parts:

Part #1 The God Part – Which is pure and flawless.

Part #2 The Human Part (us) – As the prophetic word flows through a human delivery vehicle, we must do our very best to accurately interpret and share the prophecy, but at our best we are still human.

So as it says in: *I Corinthians 14:32 (AMP) [32] for the spirits of prophets are subject to the prophets [the prophecy is under the speaker's control, and he can stop speaking];*

When God has given us revelation for someone else, He has entrusted a priceless treasure into our care: *His word.* We must jealously guard it, and then as lovingly and accurately as possible deliver that treasure to the intended person or persons. We have to deliberately and purposefully be humble throughout the whole process of prophecy from receiving revelation all the way to sharing it. Remember to honor God and give Him all the glory. Also remain open and teachable, while thankfully considering input from others.

I need to add something here. In the mid 1980's I was mentored by an amazingly anointed man of God. Anytime that someone would complement him for doing something well, he would quickly say, "To God be the glory," and the person who complimented him would just stand there, kind of smile and not know what to say. This would normally end the interaction. I did this myself for several years, but something about this just never *felt* right in my spirit. Giving God all the Glory is absolutely right, and we must be careful to do it. However, when someone is being nice to us and we do not acknowledge their kindness, we miss out on an opportunity to build relationship with them. After considerable prayer and contemplation I obtained resolution. So here is what works for me. When someone gives me a compliment, I promptly say "Thank you," and then also give credit to those who were a part of the success I enjoy. As soon as possible that day, I visit with God and whole heartedly give Him all the glory, credit and praise for anything good that happened.

Sharing Guidelines

When sharing prophetic words with someone, always adhere to Biblical guidelines. These two scriptures present healthy guidelines.

This first one governs the content

[3] *But [on the other hand] the one who prophesies speaks to people for edification [to promote their spiritual growth] and [speaks words of] encouragement [to uphold and advise them concerning the matters of God]*

and [speaks words of] consolation [to compassionately comfort them].
-1 Corinthians 14:3 (AMP)

Whatever God shared with us, we in turn must share according to this guideline.

This second one governs the person delivering

[17] But the wisdom from above is first pure [morally and spiritually undefiled], then peace-loving [courteous, considerate], gentle, reasonable [and willing to listen], full of compassion and good fruits. It is unwavering, without [self-righteous] hypocrisy [and self-serving guile]. [18] And the seed whose fruit is righteousness (spiritual maturity) is sown in peace by those who make peace [by actively encouraging goodwill between individuals]. -James 3:17-18 (AMP)

This second verse in James speaks to the person sharing His word. God has shared His wisdom from above with us. Then, we must endeavor to have and exhibit the qualities mentioned above.

> The revelation you received is never more important than loving the person it is for

So, humbly implement these Biblical guidelines when God speaks to you for yourself or for others. From us receiving God's wisdom and revelation, to sharing it, unconditional love will govern the delivery. This *love* filter causes the speaking of God's wisdom to be the rest of the verse after the *Then*. I do not believe it is possible to fully convey Father's spoken word without having Father's heart of love. The revelation you received is never more important than loving the person it is for.

Read beginning in *1 Corinthians 12:31 (NASB)*

But earnestly desire the greater gifts. And I show you a still more excellent way.

And continuing on in chapter 13 the Bible says that love is our greatest expression. Our *more excellent way* to help and serve others is by selflessly loving them.

Other helpful scriptures

Sharing prophecy is speaking to others. As such, all the Biblical guidelines that apply to speaking and using the tongue govern prophetic ministry as well. Here is a partial list of scriptures to consider and adhere to while prophesying:

Proverbs: 10:20, 10 :31, 12:18 , 15:1-2 , 15:4, 16:24, 18:24, Isaiah 50:4 and I Peter 3:10

God has been faithful to us in His word, clearly showing us how to use our mouths to love and strengthen each other.

So, we believe that we have received prophetic revelation from God to be shared with someone. We have interpreted what we received and feel that it is time to share the word with the person it is for. The appropriate means of sharing prophetic words can vary depending on the setting, your relationship with the person the word is for and your position of authority within the group. Following are general guidelines for sharing prophetic words within a church/group setting

Giving the word in a church or group setting

Respect, humility and care for the person you would like to share a prophetic word with is the first thing the hearer will sense, even more than the content of the words you speak.

Here are some things that will help show these qualities to them.

- When you share the word with the person, say, "I think, feel, sense or believe the Lord has given me a word for you." It does not have to match this phrasing exactly. Use wording that is appropriate to you.
- It is not good to say, "God gave me a word for you." The truth is, we are a human vessel. Just like all of mankind, we can fail. Saying absolute terms such as "God says," does not give room for human error from you and it does not give the hearer room to disagree with the word.
- Try to have the word recorded electronically and sent to them so they will have it for future reference.
- After sharing the word with them, ask them, "Does this word make sense, resonate, agree, or connect with you?" Again, it does not have to be exactly like this.-Put into your own words.

In a church setting, it is preferred to have the word witnessed by your peers.

What does this look like?

- The person sharing the word should have someone with them who can listen to what is shared and coach them afterward. This is often someone who has authority in the church such as a home group leader, teacher, elder or pastor. This setting creates a safe place for

- The one sharing because everything is said in the open, among peers and with the word being recorded. Anything that could have been wrong is open for coaching which will help the one sharing grow in their ability to hear from God for others.
- The one hearing the word should have someone with them who can listen to what is shared and be a second pair of ears with them. This person could be a close friend, parent, spouse or mentor. If the word resonates with both of them, it can have an even deeper impact and productivity in their life. If the person is a minor, always have a parent or guardian present when sharing a word.

At the mouth of two witnesses, or at the mouth of three witnesses, shall a matter be established.
-Deuteronomy 19:15b (WEB) see also -2 Corinthians 13:1

Some other scriptures that also speak of the value of a group are: Proverbs 11:14, Proverbs 15:22, Proverbs 19:20, Proverbs 24:6. As we see in life as well as in the scripture, there is great value in having other caring people around us to discuss things with, bounce things off of, and speak into each other's lives.

Biblical accountability looks like this:

As iron sharpens iron, So one man sharpens [and influences] another [through discussion]. -Proverbs 27:17 (AMP)

⁵ Let the righteous [thoughtfully] strike (correct) me—it is a kindness [done to encourage my spiritual maturity]. It is [the choicest anointing] oil on the head; Let my head not refuse [to accept and acknowledge and learn from] it; -Psalm 141:5 (AMP)

Taking it to the street

- In our daily life outside the church setting, try to include friends or family of the person receiving the word whenever possible. This will reinforce the word given and promote discussion between them after you are gone.
- If it is just you and the person the word is for, be polite and respectful. Deliver the word to them, encouraging them to discuss the word with a friend, family member, or church leader. Also, suggest to the person receiving the word to record it, listen to later, and write it down.

Let's look at another way to share prophetic words

The God Led Prayer

This is a different means to deliver a prophetic word. This method works well with individuals who, for whatever reason, either does not believe in prophecy or you discern that you need a less direct way to deliver the word.

The Bible says:

To the [a]weak I became [as the] weak, to win the weak. I have become all things to all men, so that I may by all means [in any and every way] save some [by leading them to faith in Jesus Christ].
-1 Corinthians 9:22 (AMP)

I included the foot note for this verse from the Amplified Bible:

a. 1 Corinthians 9:22 Paul may be talking about those with spiritually immature consciences regarding questionable issues (see ch 8). If so, he means that he abstained from any practice which he knew was actually acceptable for him, but capable of posing a bad example for others who were less mature spiritually.

And Jesus used a similar approach to connect with people by speaking to fisherman about fishing for *people*.

[18] Walking by the Sea of Galilee, he[a] saw two brothers: Simon, who is called Peter, and Andrew, his brother, casting a net into the sea; for they were fishermen. [19] He said to them, "Come after me, and I will make you fishers for men." -Matthew 4:18-19 (WEB)

There are many Christians and others who belong to various church denominations or for other reasons do not believe that prophecy is for today. If you or I were to approach them and say, "I believe that I have a prophetic word for you," They would close down to us and the prophetic word that God gave us to share with them. Then, our relationship with them could become strained. What is more important to God; our relationship with other people, Christian or not, or us sharing the prophetic word with a certain *label* on it? Of course, God wants us to share the prophecy, but He also wants to maintain and increase healthy relationships as well.

Here is where the prophetic word is delivered via the *God led Prayer*. The word does not lose its purity or meaning. It just arrives in a different package. At Christmas time children don't really care how the gift is wrapped. They just want the gift. The same holds true here. The gift or prophecy to the person is the same. We just deliver it wrapped in the most relationship strengthening package we can.

I have shared many prophetic words in this way over the years with individuals. I delivered them this way because I either believed or sensed that this was the appropriate method, or I knew the person well enough to know that this would be the most productive way to deliver the word to them.

The *God led prayer* looks like this:

You or I and the person that the revelation is for pray together, and the prophetic word is delivered or spoken during the prayer.

What is beneficial about this is after the prayer, very often the person is amazed at just how *God led* the prayer was. Things that no one knew about, but them and God, were prayed for. Specifics about where they are now and what God is doing in their lives. Also, *divine insight* about their future that really connects with them is revealed. The desires of their heart are reinforced (Psalm 37:4). Oftentimes, the God given vision for their life is strengthened through the prayer. Wow! Relationships strengthened! Word delivered! God becomes more real to them and us. And guess what else? They actually moved one step closer to believing in prophecy!

Holding onto a word until the right season

There are times when the Lord will give us revelation for someone or about someone's life, and as we consider sharing it with them, we have a hesitance in our spirit. It just doesn't *feel* right to share the revelation with them. This Holy Spirit *check* in our spirits is to be obeyed. Don't ever push through His leading in any area of life. Never quench Him (1 Thess 5:19), this includes sharing prophecy. Think about the revelation you received, pray about it, even consider sharing it at different time to see if the Holy Spirit is still saying, by His hesitancy in our spirit, not to share it. I have come to greatly appreciate His leading more and more over the years. Only God knows what is best, including when the time is right to share His spoken word with others. After all, it is His word and not ours. This holding of the word until the right season can be for many reasons.

> After all, it is His word, not ours

Some of these reasons are

- To more precisely pray for the person or group
- To encourage them at just the right moment as they work through something
- To sow financially or materially into the area that God shared with you
- To reinforce a God given call or direction in their lives
- To solidify a decision or direction that the person chooses
- To be ready to stand in agreement with them as they make decisions or changes in their lives

Here are two examples of these types of words

I was ministering to a group of young men several years ago. When I placed my hand on one of their shoulders, I saw him married. I also saw the young lady that he would marry. It was the young lady he had just begun dating. I saw an image that unfolded like a small movie clip. A *movie trailer,* so to speak, of the marriage ceremony. I saw the two of them as a happy couple. He had a good job with God's favor on his life, influence into the community and God's blessing on this marriage and their future together.

The reason not to share this first example is self-evident. This word would have been too much information at this point in his life. It would have created tremendous strain on the new relationship between him and the young lady. I included this as an example of a Holy Spirit check, but also, as a *common sense* example. Be mindful to always obey the Holy Spirit's leading.

The day came that they were married and I was able to share the word I had received two years earlier. During the time between receiving the initial revelation and the day of their marriage, I had been praying and discussing with God what He had showed me. Through this process, more revelation was received. So, when the time came to share with the couple, the confirmation of their decision was priceless, and they were greatly encouraged!

Second example

My wife and I were attending a wedding. As the vows were exchanged, I saw a small *movie trailer* of revelation about them. They were at home standing in the kitchen next to the bar. They were very happy with children playing at their feet. I could also see from inside the kitchen, out through the sliding door. The man and his wife were about the same age they appeared that day at their wedding. The view through the sliding door was of the landscape and mountains where we all currently lived. As I considered the image, there were several components of this revelation:

71

The couple was about the same age.

They were living in the same area.

They were a happy family with children, but living in a different home.

There were two areas in particular that the Holy Spirit really emphasized:

One was the setting. The view I had was as if I was standing in the corner of the kitchen, and at one moment, I could sense the Holy Spirit drawing my attention to the whole setting. The full scope, so to speak. The young couple was happy with children. And then, I looked at the kids. There was a strong, clear impression, and I heard, "These are their kids." The vision ended. I thought of sharing it with them but had a very strong *check* in my spirit. I felt like the Holy Spirit was saying, "Not now." So, I kept the word in my heart, prayed for it to come to pass in their lives and waited to see if He would have me share it at another time. I shared the word with my wife.

Several months passed. One day my wife was talking with the mother of the young man that the revelation was for. His mother said that the couple had been trying to have children with no success. She also said that they went to the doctor and after having tests, found out that they could not have children. The couple was devastated. My wife promptly connected me with the couple. I talked with the man and his wife, knowing that this was the time to share the revelation from their wedding day. They received the word, held fast to the word, and whole heartedly believed God for children. Then, you guessed it. She promptly became pregnant, had a son and then a daughter. Praise God!

God is incredible!

These examples show us more than just two prophetic words that were held until the right time. These touch on a bigger issue which is the need for all Christians to be led by the Holy Spirit. From our time with God to our interactions with other people, be sensitive to Him and also be filled with love for other people. Look to express love in all relationships and then your interactions will be purer, cleaner, and make a bigger difference. People will be safe with us and they will know it. I also believe that love is the key to hearing the Holy Spirit's voice regarding whether or not to share, pray about, or even when to give a prophetic word. Love never forces its way into another's life. It doesn't have to. Everyone is God-designed to respond to His love.

Knowledge [alone] makes [people self-righteously] arrogant, but love [that unselfishly seeks the best for others] builds up and encourages others to grow [in wisdom]. -1 Corinthians 8:1b (AMP)

> Love never forces its way into another's life

Personal Responsibility

When we receive prophetic revelation from God for someone, our responsibility is to prayerfully and meditatively interact with God until we believe we have received and interpreted the *complete* word. Sometimes the revelation received does not require interpretation. Some examples of this are: A word of knowledge that is clear and complete, like a picture, an object or a place or a statement. I have had revelation that, as soon as I received it, I knew to share it *exactly* as it was.

Example

While praying for someone, I saw an image of a large oak tree. I asked God what it meant and immediately I knew that oak trees are known for their strength. I shared with the person that God sees them like an oak tree, strong and steady. I did not know it, but they were in a place in life where they were uncertain of their strength and they were encouraged to know that God had made them strong like an oak tree. Their confidence was greatly boosted.

There are times that the interpretation is *attached* to the original revelation as a complete two part download. There are also times that prophetic words gradually unfold, having layers or pieces that come into our spirit over any length of time from seconds to minutes, even days or longer. I have had words for individuals or groups that have unfolded a piece at a time for up to several months.

Example from Cheryl:

Once, I was asked to minister prophetically to someone who was in a very difficult place. I had a week to prepare to minister and asked God what he would have me share. I immediately saw a picture of a large roast cooking in an oven and a savory smell filling the room. I had no idea what the picture meant so I assumed that I must have been praying while hungry! I continued to pray over the next several days and the image continued to come to my mind. I asked God, "What does this mean? How could this apply to her situation or connect in any way?" Over the next several days in prayer, layer upon layer of revelation about the roast became clear. When I felt the word was complete, I shared with her the image I saw. Then, I shared what I believed was God's perspective. She was like the roast in an oven. She was feeling the heat of her difficult circumstances. But in God's eyes, she was a wonderful fragrance that draws hungry people close to her. That when she is under duress, the Lords fragrance of hope is even stronger to those around her and that she draws people close to God in a unique way. Layer upon layer the word continued to unfold until I felt that God had given me a complete message for her. She was very encouraged to know that even though she could feel the heat of the trial she was in, God saw her as a wonderful fragrance to draw many hungry souls to Him.

When prophetic revelation is received, be sensitive to what is going on with what you received. When you look at, ponder, or examine it, is anything being added, changing, or expanding? Do you have a sense that you have the *complete* revelation that you need to share? Is there a sense of peace and freedom when you consider sharing the word? Do you have hesitancy or a *check* in your spirit when thinking about sharing? Do you feel peace when you look at the word and your interpretation of it?

Hearing from God is the beginning of a beautiful interaction between us and God, and then other people, if the word is for someone else. Healthy prophecy always has at its heart loving, strong, relationship. Prophecy draws people closer to their loving God and closer to other people. His word, be it written, or spoken, always builds healthy family.

> Healthy prophecy always has at it's heart loving, strong, relationship. Prophecy draws people closer to their loving God and closer to other people. His word, be it written or spoken always builds healthy family

Your Responsibility is fulfilled

When we believe we have received revelation, carefully and prayerfully interpreted it, believe it is time to share, and then we share the word with the person, group or leadership of a group, our responsibility before God is fulfilled. What the person or leadership do with the word after that is their responsibility. It is between them and God. Our obligation is fulfilled. In a sense, we are the delivery person for a priceless treasure and when we hand over the treasure to the right person, it is no longer our responsibility. The word is theirs to care for. We are like an armored carrier that picks up the money from a bank. We guard and protect the treasure and take personal responsibility for it until it is delivered.

I have witnessed individuals struggle with this truth over the years. The person would receive a prophetic word that was for someone else, share the word with them and then they would regularly *check in* with them about their progress with the word. They wanted a detailed report of the progress. I have seen this happen between Christians and other Christians. I have also seen this many times between Christians who shared the word and church leadership, Pastors or Elders.

> The power of choice is one of the greatest gifts given to mankind.

While caring about others is good and a measure of accountability is healthy, we each know that it is impossible to manipulate and control someone else's life. It is also just plain wrong to try and control others. The power of choice is one of the greatest gifts given to mankind.

Healthy accountability is based on healthy relationships. Control is based on expectations, not relationship. Let each of us remember that only the person the revelation is for can properly integrate it into their life.

Testimony

The Lord engrained this truth in me in 1989. I was in the Army and had been sharing Jesus with many other soldiers. Some trusted Christ and some didn't. I was sitting up in my bunk praying and crying. I was terribly upset that people were rejecting Jesus and I felt as if they were rejecting me as well. As I continued to pray and cry, I clearly heard the Lord say to me, "You are not responsible for their response. You are only responsible to be obedient." This set me free! Those words brought a healthy ability in me to share Jesus and release the responsibility to the other person. I continued to witness, but with greater freedom. I still cared deeply for those I spoke with, but I did not feel guilty every time someone rejected Christ or got upset with me for being and acting like a Christian.

> Healthy accountability is based on healthy relationships.
>
> Control is based on expectations, not relationship

Interesting responses

I have given prophetic words to individuals over the years and on occasion, I have had a person look at me and say, "I don't agree with that word," or some other phrase saying basically the same thing. When this has happened, I look at the person and say, "Thank you for letting me share with you. Maybe I was wrong." If the word was accurate, God will validate it in them during their devotions, someone else or by some other means.

I have also had people disagree with a prophetic word, while at the same time, the friends and family with them are agreeing with the word. I get amused when this happens as often those around us see us more clearly than we see ourselves. I sometimes have difficulty not smiling or laughing, as that could appear disrespectful. I know that there will be some great conversations following! It is not about me or you being completely right. It is about each one of us being obedient. The truth is that all of us who dearly love God, at the end of the day, have tried our very best to honor God and love people. And not one of us is perfect. Everyone can and does make mistakes and that is ok. In fact, it is perfectly normal. This realization is vital to help keep us dependent on Jesus and stay relevant to people. This reality also helps us remain accountable and open to input from others. See Ecclesiastes 4:9-12

Just because a person disagrees with a word shared, does not necessarily mean that the word is inaccurate.

Testimony

An example of this comes from my past. Many years ago, my wife and I had relocated to North Carolina and were attending a church there. One day an elder approached me and said, "I have a word for you and your wife." I said, "That is great!" Then, we proceeded to connect with one of the pastors, and all four of us went into an office where the elder shared the word with my wife and I. We fully agreed with the first part of the word. But, then he shared the second part of the word, which was, "I believe the Lord is going to move you and your family from here to another place soon." I looked at my wife and she was becoming pale. She looked upset. I could feel her emotions spiking. I politely let him finish. I thanked him for sharing, and then said to him, "I agree with the first part of the word, but I disagree with the part of the word that said that my family and I will be moving soon." I looked over at my wife and noticed that she was ever so slightly starting to relax. We did end up moving six years later. Not *soon*.

When I disagreed with the *moving soon* part of the word, I was not really sure if the word was accurate or not. What I was sure of was that my wife needed my support/protection at that moment. What no one there other than my wife and I knew was how difficult of a move we had just made to NC. We had left many close friends and our church family. We had only been in NC for a few months. We had not even fully unpacked our things. We were filled with hope for our new home. Wanting to root in and establish healthy relationships. By me disagreeing, my wife felt safe. She knew that we were still going to have unity and keep working together toward the goals we believed God had given us.

After the meeting, God and I visited in prayer alone and I shared with Him my appreciation for the prophetic word that day. I also discussed the reasons for my response to the elder sharing the word. And that I was open to any leading from Him. The Holy Spirit gave me a strong peace. I felt He was happy with the way I had responded. About four years later, God confirmed the *moving* part of the word with my wife and me at just the right time. God brought everything together and after two more years, we relocated.

You may be thinking, "Why would you disagree with a word from God to support your wife?" The answer is that my wife and I had for the previous two or three years sought God together and in unity with His leading, put a plan together for us and our family. My wife and I also knew that we would be in NC. for a *season* as God had placed that on our hearts. So, we knew that we would move eventually, but not *soon.*

I also know that God is not the author of division, but unity and love. His and my love for my wife is more important than any gift or expression, even prophecy. I kept the word in my heart because I felt that it would happen eventually. And you can be sure that for a while, I did not speak of relocating with my wife but prayed for God to reveal it to her directly at the perfect moment, and have her bring it up with me. In time, she did. The truth to each one of us is that our relationship with God and others is bigger, more expansive, and more beautiful than any single prophetic word.

Prophetic words that require caution

Some of these types of words are touched on throughout the book.

A word of correction

You are doing this wrong. You need to stop or repent.

Why? We do not have that level of authority in another person's life. Unless it is our child or a person we are responsible for. To correct another person can be a form of control. Giving correction as a friend or parent is different than saying, "I believe God is telling me to correct you." This type of word can be a form of manipulation and control.

Or do you think lightly of the riches of His kindness and tolerance and patience, not knowing that the kindness of God leads you to repentance?
-Romans 2:4

A word of direction

I believe God is telling me you will: change jobs, relocate, change church, do this or that with your family etc..

Why? Again, this can be a form of manipulation or control. Free will is one of God's greatest gifts. The opportunity to partner with God in prayer and have a journey of faith with Him can be the most fulfilling part of our life. If a person changes the direction of their life based on your prophetic word and things go terribly wrong, you played a part in that. When we say, "I believe God is saying, go *here* or do *this*," we put *God* on the decision. The person hearing the word can feel guilty if they don't act, whether they have peace or not.

Dates or Timelines

Something will happen before the year is out. Your breakthrough is within the month. At the end of school, you will experience great success.

Why? All of these are examples of creating a timeline for God to meet. And if or when this timeline is not met, the person is let down. It is better to not indicate any time. Saying, at some point in the future is much better than soon, next month, the end of the season, or year.

Mates

We are not matchmakers.

Why? If you see someone together, speaking it to them can put a lot of pressure on them to become a couple instead of letting them navigate the relationship on their own.

We have to walk out any prophetic word we receive. In the big picture, words are easy to share and easy to hear, but often, HARD to WALK out. Be careful with what is shared with people because they are the ones who will carry the word to completion with the help of the Holy Spirit.

This is a very intimate and sometimes difficult journey. Our place on their path is to provide encouragement, stability, love and grace.

Be very careful with these types of words. Sometimes, God will give these words so we can pray for the person and share it with them as a confirmation after the word has come to pass. Also, there are times when these words need to be shared immediately. If you believe God wants you to share this type of word, seek the counsel of leaders around you before sharing the word with the intended recipient. These types of words carry a lot of weight and have a great potential to hurt the one hearing it.

What to do with what you hear from God

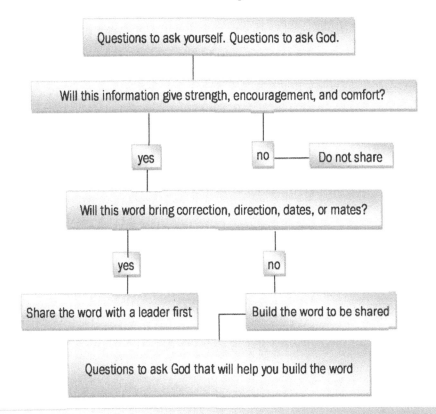

Questions to ask yourself. Questions to ask God.

Will this information give strength, encouragement, and comfort?

yes

no — Do not share

Will this word bring correction, direction, dates, or mates?

yes

no

Share the word with a leader first

Build the word to be shared

Questions to ask God that will help you build the word

- What is this?

- What does it mean?

- What is happening?

- How does this connect with them?

- What part of them are you touching, God?

- What is this word giving them? Comfort, encouragement, peace, mercy, faith strength, boldness or something else?

- Do I share this or pray about it?

- What do I share?

- What is the best time to share?

- Will I need to move in opposites?

- If yes, what is the best way to move in opposites?

- What are you doing in their life, God?

- God, is there anything in their life you are going to do in the future?

- God, is there anything they can do to be closer to you in the days ahead?

- God, what are you going to do to help them in their life?

- Are there any words from the Bible that connect with this word?

- How do I need to share this word? Loud or soft

- What emotion should be in my speaking? Boldness, gentle, excitement, joy, happy, sad, tears or strength

CHAPTER 3

Prophetic Process

New Things

The Time Test

Fighting With Your Prophecies

New things

If you or I receive a prophetic word that speaks of something new, or something that does not seem to fit into what you believe God has been saying to you, or it speaks of changing directions with your life or plans suddenly, be responsible. Please do not just receive a word that is new and radically adjust your life goals in pursuit of fulfilling the word. Prayerfully visit with God about the word. *Meditate* or *ponder* the word.

Years ago I read somewhere that to meditate is the same process that a cow does while eating its food. The cow gets a mouthful of food, chews it thoroughly, then, swallows it, allowing it to go into the stomach and mix with the digestive juices, thereby breaking the food down. The cow then brings it back up to the mouth and repeats this process a few times, getting as much nutrition out of the food as possible. This is the same process we need to do when we meditate upon God's word, written or spoken. We should allow plenty of time for the word to be *sifted* between us and God. It is also good to ask others you trust to pray with you about the word. You do not have to give those praying every detail, as they are not always needed.

God will give you adequate time to discuss the word with Him, time to get wise counsel and time for validation through others. He loves partnering with us and helping us sort things out. The devil and our ego, *selfishness,* will try to push, pull and jerk us around; telling us that we must do it right now or else, because we don't want to miss out on anything. With God, there is always an appropriate time to do things. But it is out of rest and freedom. Learning to pro-actively follow His peace is priceless. We shouldn't be reacting out of a sense of crises or fear of missing out.

> The devil and our ego will try to push, pull, and jerk us around, telling us that we must do it right now or else.

The Time Test

My wife and I have a time test for any new prophecy, personal plans, or opportunities of which we are unsure. We will commit to pray and discuss the idea or plan with God for a set number of days and see if it stays strong or increases in potency. What we have found is that if it is God-given, it has all the power to stand on its own. For God's word is living and powerful Hebrews 4:12, and will not return void Isaiah 55:11.

When a prophetic word, or any plan or Goal is not from God, but of human origin or from Satan, it will not stand up to prolonged scrutiny, sifting or prayerful consideration as it has limited power. It only has the power we give it. Even if it originated with Satan, he can only give us the word or idea. It is up to us to feed it and care for it if it is to live and grow.

As we engage with God and seek His will, asking His counsel about the revelation, word or plan, things of God will increase and natural or carnal things will decrease. God has built into every word and every plan of

His enough time to connect with Him and sort out enough of His will to take the next step. God's desire for us is not to procrastinate, but also not to foolishly rush off in our own strength. He gives us just the right amount of time to partner with the Holy Spirit, pray about it and discuss it with other people who genuinely care for us. God gives us time to submit it to caring leaders for input and time to make good, solid decisions based on His will. Boy is this good advice! If only I could have had, and would have listened to this, in my younger years.

> Proactively follow His peace

Don't make big decisions based on one prophetic word, unless the word connects with and builds on things, visions or plans in your heart that you and God have already been discussing.

For a great example of this let's have a look at Paul the apostle and how he responded to prophecy he received. In Acts 21:3-4 Paul had just gotten off of a ship in the city of Tyre. He connected with some disciples who prophesied to him. They pleaded with him *not* to go up to Jerusalem. There is no recorded response to this prophecy here. But let's keep looking, as this is only one of the times this prophecy was given to Paul. Next in Acts 21:8-14 Agabus prophesies to Paul that in Jerusalem he will be bound and delivered to the Gentiles. The disciples and others there begged Paul *not* to go to Jerusalem. Paul did not change his mind about going there, even after being warned of what awaited him. Why would Paul continue on to a place when God had warned him that he would have hardship when he arrived? Let's look at some scriptures that help us understand Paul's resolve:

²¹ And the Lord said to me, 'Go, I will send you far away to the Gentiles.'
-Acts 22:21 (AMP)

" On the following night the Lord stood near Paul and said, "Be brave; for as you have solemnly and faithfully witnessed about Me at Jerusalem, so you must also testify at Rome." -Acts 23:11 (AMP)

And Acts 20:22-24 makes it clear why Paul stayed his course, even after several prophecies that those around him believed to be a warning for him *not* to continue on to Jerusalem.

Let's have a closer look at what was really going on in Paul. In verse 23 Paul says that in every city he had received prophetic words about what was going to happen to him.

Acts 20:24 is the key.

²⁴ But I do not consider my life as something of value or dear to me, so that I may [with joy] finish my course and the ministry which I received from the Lord Jesus, to testify faithfully of the good news of God's [precious, undeserved] grace [which makes us free of the guilt of sin and grants us eternal life]. -Acts 20:24 Amplified Bible (AMP)

Paul knew that God had called him to go to Jerusalem and to the Gentiles. He knew that he was on track with God and he was going to continue following his God, no matter what happened. The people around him only saw tribulation and difficulty. Paul saw that God was prophetically giving him helpful details for the next part of his journey. That's how prophecy is: It is to help us on our journey with God. Only the person the prophecy is for can really understand how and where to integrate the prophetic words they receive into their lives. When we share a prophetic word with someone, it is their responsibility to steward their word, discuss it with God, and then for God and them work it into and out of their life appropriately. It is up to each of us after we trust Christ to work out our own salvation with fear and trembling -Philippians 2:12-13. Our

Prophetic Process

relationship with God is bigger, more expansive, more full of love and life, than any prophetic word can contain.

The Bible says

⁹ For we know in part, and we prophesy in part [for our knowledge is fragmentary and incomplete]. -1 Corinthians 13:9(AMP)

Any prophetic word is only a part. A very helpful and needed part of a person's incredible, ever expanding, ever-changing, beautiful life. But, it is still only a part.

When someone shares a prophetic word with us, the way we respond to the word is very important. So please give the person sharing with you your undivided attention, listen carefully and If possible, record the word as it is being shared. If you cannot record the word, write it down promptly, every word and every detail of it. Take responsibility for your prophetic words. Do not ignore them, neglect them, shelve them or otherwise become disengaged with them. Regularly express thankfulness to God for them. We must partner with God in our prophecies to see them fully realized.

Be like Jacob in Genesis 32:24-30. When things are tough, wrestle with God like Jacob did until you are blessed. This wrestling with God may sound selfish, but it's really not. Jacob new that God's plans for him were good and would also bless many, many others. That's not selfish. Don't let your faith for their fulfillment cool down. Be like Jacob and don't let go of your loving God until he blesses you! I know this may sound intense and pushy with God. But, if our heart is to know and serve Him more effectively and to help others with everything He gives us, then go for it! Pray about, pray through, have regular Q and A with God. Ask and keep on asking! Sometimes you will need to wrestle with God, but more often with yourself.

91

A great scripture that conveys this relentless pursuit of God and His blessing is:

[12] From the days of John the Baptist until now the kingdom of heaven suffers violent assault, and violent men seize it by force [as a precious prize].
-Matthew 11:12 (AMP)

The key in all of this is relationship. We cannot do anything good alone, and God will not do everything for us. It is a partnership. So when we receive a prophetic word, believe it and mix our faith with it. We will then be catapulted into a season of transformation. His word will test us. It will require considerable change in us.

A great example of what happens in us is

[12] And Jesus entered the temple and drove out all those who were buying and selling in the temple, and overturned the tables of the money changers and the seats of those who were selling doves. [13] And He *said to them, "It is written, 'My house shall be called a house of prayer'; but you are making it a robbers' den." -Matthew 21:12-13 (NASB)

In this scripture in Matthew, Jesus, the living word, goes into a natural temple and drives out everything selfish. This is an exact picture of the process that takes place in the life of a believer. We trust Jesus as our Lord and Father God sends the Holy Spirit to dwell in us. And then He begins to separate and drive out the things in our lives that hurt us and keep us in bondage. Things that separate us from our God and the limitless treasures we are meant to enjoy.

The same process takes place when we receive a God given Prophetic word, dream or vision. His Spoken word comes into our *temple, meaning our heart, 1Corinthians 6:19* and separates the things of God in us

92

from the things of the natural man, the flesh, soul and selfishness. See *Hebrews 4:12.* This ongoing separation and driving things of the flesh to the surface so that together we and the Holy Spirit can deal with them is called sanctification. It is the beautiful process of progressively submitting every area of our lives to Jesus' Lordship. This refining is required for God to express Himself through us in ever increasing amounts. Practically speaking, the more of our temple the Holy Spirit has control of, the greater His expression through us. This process is a necessary part of each Christian's life. However, when we receive a prophecy, the Holy Spirit will often begin to focus His life changing attention on *specific* areas that must be yielded to Jesus' Lordship. Areas in us that must change for the fulfillment of God's unique call on the person's life. The Holy Spirit does this so that He can fully inhabit those parts of us and express Himself through us as He desires. I cannot tell you how many times I have witnessed someone receive a prophetic word and then they are promptly catapulted into a season of intense change.

As the Bible says

[6] *'Not by might nor by power, but by My Spirit,' says the Lord of hosts.*
-Zechariah 4:6b (NASB)

[10] *"But He knows the way that I take [and He pays attention to it]. When He has tried me, I will come forth as [refined] gold [pure and luminous]. -Job 23:10 Amplified Bible (AMP)*

Also see how Joseph's word tested him:

[19] *Until the time that his word [of prophecy regarding his brothers] came true, the word of the Lord tested and refined him.*
-Psalm 105:19 (AMP)

For many great examples of people who had God-given dreams, prophecies and calls on their life, people who believed in God and fully partnered with him, staying faithful to Jesus through whatever He led them through, read Hebrews chapter 11.

Fighting with Your Prophecies

Paul said to Timothy:

[18] This command I entrust to you, Timothy, my son, in accordance with the prophecies previously made concerning you, that by them you fight the good fight, -1 Timothy 1:18 (NASB)

Another important part of our partnering with God in our destinies is to fight with our prophecies.

Why do we fight with our prophecies?

[24] Do you not know that in a race all the runners run [their very best to win], but only one receives the prize? Run [your race] in such a way that you may seize the prize and make it yours! [25] Now every athlete who [goes into training and] competes in the games is disciplined and exercises self-control in all things. They do it to win a crown that withers, but we [do it to receive] an imperishable [crown that cannot wither]. [26] Therefore I do not run without a definite goal; I do not flail around like one beating the air [just shadow boxing]. [27] But [like a boxer] I strictly discipline my body and make it my slave, so that, after I have preached [the gospel] to others, I myself will not somehow be disqualified [as unfit for service]. -1 Corinthians 9:24-27 (AMP)

While all Christians should have an ever increasing desire to know Him & daily refine our character into His image, we also have the same responsibility to reach the lost for Jesus, be honest, have integrity and steward the things that God has entrusted to us.

His call on each life is unique. God has specific plans. A custom designed destiny for each of His children. This is why we fight with our prophecies. The uniqueness of our destiny requires it. Looking back at verse 26 again, prophecies combined with God given vision gives us clear goals to run to. This clarity greatly helps us to not flail around and wear ourselves out *"beating the air" vs 26*. We fight with our prophecies so that we can redeem the time and finish our specific God given, God glorifying course.

How do we "fight" with our Prophecies?

Along our journey through this natural life all of us will enjoy good times. We will also face hardships and difficulties. Everyone goes through these times and seasons. Christians, when we know through God given vision and prophetic revelation His plans for our lives, we in the truest sense have a lighthouse that shines clearly enough to be seen by day and shines even brighter by night when life is dark or foggy. If that alone wasn't good enough, God in His kindness never turns the light off! No matter what the *weather* condition of our lives is.

Remember how God led the children of Israel through their wilderness through the cloud by day and the fire by night. See Exodus 13:21-22. By day when everything around them was clearly visible and by night when they could not see the right way to go, they had a visible means to keep their focus in the right direction. The children of Israel were led by the cloud and the fire, visions of a better life and also by God's consistent spoken revelation through Moses the prophet every step of the way into their promises.

As we follow God closely and by vision and prophetic revelation do our very best to stay on the right course, there will be times of difficulty. And our view of these hardships and struggles will become different. Knowing we are *on track* makes it much easier to transform these experiences into opportunities to connect with God in them and grow spiritually. As our steps are ordered by the Lord, *Psalm 37:23*, everything we encounter on our path has contained within it God designed *upgrades*.

[28] *And we know [with great confidence] that God [who is deeply concerned about us] causes all things to work together [as a plan] for good for those who love God, to those who are called according to His plan and purpose.* -Romans 8:28 (AMP)

Let's pull this teaching together. The way we fight with our prophecies in day to day life, a hardship, struggle or other stressful situation is to:

1. Whenever you encounter something, ask God how this specific experience connects with the vision and prophetic revelation you have for your life.

2. See each experience in life, even hardship and difficulty, as training or equipping for the next step of your journey and ultimately a needed experience to fulfill your call.

3. Look for God in the midst of trials, not the devil.

4. Pro-actively give God thanks and praise for the upgrade He was kind enough to personally send you. No matter what the package it comes in looks or feels like.

5. When things are not lining up how you think they should, ask God for understanding. Encourage yourself in the Lord as David did. -*I Samuel 30:6.* Remind yourself of the vision you have for your life. Declare, out loud, the prophetic promises, convictions, vision and destiny you have.

6. Humble yourself before the Lord and ask Him to create a path through your trial. Ask Him to help you see Him clearly in your situation.

7. Ask God if anything in your heart or vision for your life needs to be adjusted to better walk the path before you.

8. Ask God if there is a lie you are believing about your life and is there a truth He has for you to replace that lie.

Testimony

My wife and I along with a team went to the Philippines. The morning just before we left for the airport, I went to the basement to get my clothes out of the dryer. Upon reaching the bottom of the stairs and turning the corner into the laundry area, I saw water on the floor. I walked a few more steps and there was a lot of water on the floor! I had to leave for the airport in one hour. I looked at the water, paused briefly, smiled and said *upgrade*! I proceeded to thank God for whatever good thing I would receive out of this event. I praised Him for using this to strengthen His call on my life. I included some of the specifics of my call that had been revealed by

> "We all see what we want to see." If you train yourself to look for God and His treasure in the events, relationships, and day to day happenings in your life, I assure you that you will find Him.

prophecy in this thanks and praise. While I was talking with God I was fixing the leak. And all was resolved with a few minutes to spare.

I know this approach to hardship can seem unrealistic. But how much good do you or I get when we become stressed out and say or do negative things that do not honor God, and then destroy the potential benefit that these *upgrade moments* have hidden within them. I have a saying, We all see what we want to see. If you train yourself to look for God and His treasure in the events, relationships and day to day happenings in your life, I assure you that you will find Him.

Testimony

About 4 years ago one of my sons became quite sick, it was very sudden. One day he was well and the next he was running a high fever and complaining of lower abdominal pain. Our family and many friends prayed for him, but his condition continued to worsen. We took him to our local hospital. He was admitted immediately, his pain level and fever continued to increase. The physicians ran a multitude of tests with no specific cause identified. By the second day his fever had risen dangerously high. The physicians were doing everything they could to reduce the fever with no effect. We continued to pray for him, but the fever still did not break. As I was leaning on the bed praying with my hand on my son, the Holy Spirit reminded me of some of the prophecies spoken regarding my son's future. I immediately stood up and began to thank God for His words and plans regarding my son's future. I was *very specific,* speaking and declaring the things the prophecies said that he would do in the future. Things my son had not yet accomplished. After about a couple of minutes of this *fighting with my son's prophecies,* the fever broke and went down to normal. The fever did not cause him any more problems after that.

This brings us to another important responsibility: Fighting for other people with their prophecies. As a minister, friend, husband, parent, and grandparent, I pray for each member of my family and many others. I also fight for them with their prophecies. When we speak and declare Gods plans for our friends and family, we add our faith to theirs. Thus, greatly helping them obtain their promises. Parents in particular have tremendous authority to bless their children and grandchildren. And spouses, no other human on earth has the God given right or power to bless your mate as you do.

Testimony

I served in the military for several years, serving in Desert Storm/Shield. About one year after returning home from the war, I was driving in my car when all at once my vision went very blurry. I went back to my house and over the next few months things continued to get worse, with many other health problems arising in my body. After abundant prayer with no improvement in my condition, I went to the Veteran's Affairs V.A. Hospital for treatment. I was diagnosed with Gulf War Syndrome. The illness was terrible. After about eight months with no improvement, I was in prayer and the Holy Spirit said to me that I had to forgive the Government and the Military. He showed me that I blamed them for my sickness. So, I wholeheartedly prayed and forgave them.

Then, shortly after, during prayer, I had a vision of Jesus being whipped with the scourge. In the vision, I could see as each lash of the scourge tore open Jesus's flesh and His blood came out. I heard the Holy Spirit say as I watched this that every stripe that the scourge opened up on Jesus's back represented a specific group of sicknesses and diseases and that as Jesus's blood came out of each stripe, the sickness and disease was cleansed. As I saw this in my mind, I recalled this scripture:

⁵ But He was wounded for our transgressions,
He was crushed for our wickedness [our sin, our injustice, our wrongdoing];
The punishment [required] for our well-being fell on Him, And by His
stripes (wounds) we are healed.
-Isaiah 53:5(AMP) (Also see 1Peter 2:24)

I had been praying for healing. Every day I had been speaking and declaring healing scriptures over myself and this was one of my favorite healing scriptures. But now the Holy Spirit had given me the revelation that I needed to boost my faith and also what I needed to fight. With this revelation I fought daily. Every time I spoke this scripture I could see that image of Jesus. It was only a few months later that God in His kindness miraculously healed me. Praise God! According to the Bible, it is God's will to heal. I don't know or understand God's ways regarding healing. Some people he heals instantly, some are healed days, months, years or a lifetime later. I have seen those healed through the medicine and treatment of a doctor or naturopath. And I have seen people only healed when they die and are in the Lord's presence. In this instance, healing came to me after months. One thing I know. God is with you as you pray and fight with the God given vision you have for your life and He will meet you in that place no matter how difficult your trial may be, whether physical, emotional, or circumstantial.

When God gives revelation it is always to strengthen and empower us right where we need it so that we can little by little inhabit our promises and make the most of the life that the Lord has given us. God has given Christians two sources of unlimited power to mix with our faith and fight with: God's written word, the *Bible* and His spoken word, *Prophecy or Revelation.*

So...

How bad do you want your destiny? Parents how about your children's? Are you willing to fight for it? If your answer is yes, how long are you willing to stand on His promises and fight? It may take days, month's years or even a lifetime. But, know this for certain; it is worth it for yourself, your family, your friends, and also future generations.

But those who wait for the Lord [who expect, look for, and hope in Him]
Will gain new strength and renew their power;
They will lift up their wings [and rise up close to God] like eagles [rising
toward the sun]; They will run and not become weary, They will walk and
not grow tired.
-Isaiah 40:31(AMP) See also Psalm 27:14

CHAPTER 4

Prophetic Development

First Expression

Mistakes

Coaching

First Expression

Think back to the first time you tried something. The first time you played a sport or practiced a musical instrument or maybe that new job. Whenever we first express ourselves in any new endeavor, it is a time of learning and discovery. With experience and mentoring or training from someone who has been doing it longer, we become competent and successful. The same is true in our lives as Christians. We trust Christ and enter a whole new life. We begin living a dual citizenship. This new life as a Christian is so much more than any of us expect! We learn the beauty of partnering with the Holy Spirit in the process of change in our own lives. We also learn to recognize and respond to God's voice in our lives. This takes a great deal of time with God and encouragement from those around us, particularly leaders.

Over the years I have noticed that some of the most gifted people who are in the early stages of their Christian development can be some of the most difficult people to work with. This is because these dynamic, gifted individuals have to be mentored, trained, and developed. This can be quite challenging. It takes a lot of time and deliberate effort to disciple someone. Also, the strong, gifted, *young* Christian has to be open and willing to partner with the mentor in the process for it to work. Some people will be mentored. Some will not. I have known many who were unwilling to be *formally* mentored, but even as the hardest stone is shaped by the constant influence of water, almost anyone can be *gradually* mentored or coached through God's leading and deliberate, caring interactions with others.

> Leaders, we cannot manage someone to maturity

A word to leaders

Leaders, we cannot manage someone to maturity. However, we can consistently mentor, train, and coach people. We do this by reinforcing the good in their life. By reinforcing God in their life. All while lovingly and patiently helping them through their struggles. This is making disciples as Jesus commissioned us to. And yes, it is work. It is a lot of work and a labor of love. It is also essential as it helps others become all God created them to be.

Testimony

My wife and I led a team to the Philippines. While there the team conducted two prophetic training seminars and ministered prophetically to many people. One of the biggest highlights was that after two hours of training on how to recognize God's voice a young lady enthusiastically and with tears said, "I heard God's voice! I heard God's voice!"

Oh, the beauty of first expression!

When the Holy Spirit begins to express himself through someone in a gift or ability, the person doesn't just want to express the gift. They really, really, really, need to express what the Holy Spirit wants them to.

Jeremiah the prophet tried to hold back. Let's look at his experience:

⁹ If I say, "I will not remember Him
Or speak His name anymore,"
Then my heart becomes a burning fire
Shut up in my bones.
And I am weary of enduring and holding it in;
I cannot endure it [nor contain it any longer].
-Jeremiah 20:9 (AMP)

When a Christian holds back any area of their life from God, or from expressing what God wants to express through them, the Holy Spirit will be quenched. If the person persists and does not yield to Him, His fire and passion in that area of their life will eventually be put out. This concept is not just for prophecy but all spiritual gifts or expressions.

³⁰ And do not grieve the Holy Spirit of God [but seek to please Him], by whom you were sealed and marked [branded as God's own] for the day of redemption [the final deliverance from the consequences of sin].
-Ephesians 4:30 (AMP)

¹⁹ Do not quench [subdue, or be unresponsive to the working and guidance of] the [Holy] Spirit. -I Thessalonians 5:19 (AMP)

Anything Doesn't Just Go

Please do not use this as a license for an *Anything Goes* style of ministry. What I mean by an Anything Goes style of ministry is when you believe you have a word from God and you think the church needs to immediately make room for your word and put your God given direction on the front burner of the church's agenda. This type of thinking is selfish and full of pride.

Would you go into the home of a friend and start telling the parents and children how they should talk or behave like a good family? That would be silly. The parents are the ones responsible to feed the children and raise them according to their direction. It is the same with a church setting. The leaders in a church are in authority and responsible to God for what happens to the congregation that is under their care. It is their responsibility to ensure that ministry is done decently and in order -1 Corinthians 14:40. Their interpretation of what decently and in order means in that church group must be respected.

While this chapter is an encouragement to all Christians to respond inwardly to God and outwardly to express what the Holy Spirit has entrusted to them, it is also geared toward leaders. It is my desire to encourage leaders to faithfully coach and equip those under your care, helping those entrusted to you to become all Jesus wants them to be.

Let's see how the apostle Paul coached Timothy

14 Do not neglect the spiritual gift within you, [that special endowment] which was intentionally bestowed on you [by the Holy Spirit] through prophetic utterance when the [a]elders laid their hands on you [at your ordination]. [15] *Practice and work hard on these things; be absorbed in them [completely occupied in your ministry], so that your progress will be evident to all.* - I Timothy 4:14-15 (AMP)

Peter also says it well

[10] *Just as each one of you has received a special gift [a spiritual talent, an ability graciously given by God], employ it in serving one another as [is appropriate for] good stewards of God's multi-faceted grace [faithfully using the diverse, varied gifts and abilities granted to Christians by God's unmerited favor].* -1 Peter 4:10 (AMP)

When we see God expressing Himself in our lives or others' lives in any way, be it a gift, or ability. Celebrate the kindness of God, and rejoice with those who rejoice.

Mistakes

Let's begin with a scenario: a nine-year-old boy wants to snowboard. His father, who dearly loves him, gives him a new snowboard, and the boy is so excited to receive it! The father is excited as well, and encourages his child to use it soon. So the child, his father, mother, sister and brother discuss the new snowboard. The child in excitement says I want to use it now! The father schedules a day for the child to go snowboarding. The father will not be able to physically be there as he has a business meeting. So the father trusts the family to care for, and protect the child while he is learning to snowboard.

The family, all except the father, loads up into the car and they drive to the base of Mount Everest. The mother has reserved a helicopter to fly the nine-year-old boy and his new snowboard to the highest summit that is accessible. The child is very unsure as he thinks about what is happening. But, he so badly wants to snowboard. So he gets on the helicopter, flies high onto the mountain, gets out and comes to the edge. The child clips on his new snowboard and down he goes, with his family below watching his every move through a telescope. The boy makes it a few feet and crashes. The family is terribly disappointed. They look at him lying there, way up on the Mountain. He is just lying there, needing help, having no idea of what to do. After some time the Family, still very disappointed, sends the helicopter back up the mountain to get the child. He is picked up and flown back to his family.

As soon as the child is off the flight and approaches his family, the family proceeds to correct him and point out everything he did wrong. The small child is shocked. Thinking, "I thought my family would help me and be more supportive. After all, I tried my best. Why did my family expect me to be able to snowboard perfectly down this huge mountain anyway? I didn't know what I was doing. This snowboarding thing stinks! I would rather just get along with my family." The child's father, upon hearing the news, was moved with compassion for the child and disappointed by the mistreatment from the family. The father tries to comfort and console the child, but the child is deeply wounded by his family's treatment. The father says to himself, "I will give my child some time to recover."

The child may or may not recover. This is the case with many Christians who are mistreated by their Christian family. Some do recover and continue moving forward with God, continuing to mature. Some are wounded so deeply that they choose not to use their God given gifts or abilities. Others choose not to continue to pursue the call on their life. Some are so disappointed with their family that they prematurely launch out and *go it solo*. They leave their church family behind but carry all the hurt and disappointment with them. Leaving in their wake hurt and disappointment. I have witnessed all of these responses. Myself being one of the ones who by God's grace recovered. The scenario of the young child and the snowboard was fiction. But, it very accurately portrays how many Christians are treated as God begins to express new things in and through their lives.

Father God, by the Holy Spirit, gives gifts and abilities to each of His children. These expressions are to share His love with the church, and the world. This is a beautiful thing. God providing everything we need to be strong and healthy! To craft and adorn a bride fit for the King! When the Holy Spirit decides to express God's heart through Christians, we are all very much like the little boy with the snowboard. We get excited and have to try out what Father has given us. And just like the little boy, we don't really know what to do or how to use the gift or ability in a healthy, loving way. When we first began to prophesy, as with any other gift or expression, our heart may be right with God and our motive as pure as possible, but we are still going to make mistakes. And that is OK! In fact, it is perfectly normal. Not one of us in the beginning of any new expression or pursuit gets everything right. Even seasoned ministers with decades of experience still make mistakes. In fact, all of us do and that's why the Bible says He gives us more grace and His mercies are new each morning. Knowing that each of us will make mistakes does several great things. It keeps us in a healthy position with God and it promotes openness and accountability with others. It also helps keep us *real*. There is a tendency in all of us to expect perfection. Often, we place this unhealthy expectation on ourselves and others. There's a huge difference between expecting perfection, like the child's family in the scenario and striving to serve God with excellence. When we expect perfection we are in a sense, eliminating or greatly reducing God's grace in the lives of ourselves and others. Expecting perfection is trying to place someone back under the law.

Very much like the Pharisees did in *Matthew 23:4 (AMP)*[1] *The scribes and Pharisees tie up heavy loads [that are hard to bear] and place them on men's shoulders, but they themselves will not lift a finger [to make them lighter].*

> The only way to get experience is to get experience

We must readily and quickly have grace for others. Not judgment based on their lack of perfection. Be quick to encourage and praise them for trying. If you are the one who makes a mistake, freely admit it. Take responsibility for your mistakes, ask for forgiveness when needed and strive to improve yourself. But please do not stop being who God created you to be. Over time and with God's help, you will make fewer and fewer mistakes. The only way to get experience is to get experience and that takes time, some mistakes, and lots and lots of helpful input from the Lord and others. There have been many times while trying my very best that I have made mistakes. Later in prayer, the Holy Spirit and I would talk and He would show me what the mistake was and how I can improve. I have also made mistakes and had friends, family members, or leaders speak into my life and help me grow. Quite often the Holy Spirit and I laugh at my best effort and the huge gap between my effort and His wisdom. I would like to emphasize that the Holy Spirit has never been harsh, mean, or nasty with me over a mistake I made when my heart was right, and I was sincerely trying to honor God. I promise you that He will treat you the same way.

⁵ If any of you lacks wisdom [to guide him through a decision or circumstance], he is to ask of [our benevolent] God, who gives to everyone generously and without rebuke or blame, and it will be given to him. -James 1:5 (AMP)

So when, *not if,* you or someone else around you makes a mistake, respond with love and genuine care. Treat others as you want to be treated. Love others as you love yourself. Mistakes always become upgrades to a person's character when handled the right way. There are no small victories in a child of God's life. Every victory is huge and everyone is significant. So make the most of every mistake. In closing this section, always be nice to yourself and others, and pat yourself and others on the back much more often.

> Mistakes always become upgrades to a person's character when handled the right way. There are no small victories in a child of God's life.

Coaching

For prophetic people to reach their full potential, coaching is absolutely necessary. Many areas of Christian life can and will benefit greatly from coaching and accountability. But for individuals moving in and speaking prophetically, it absolutely must be done. Prophecy has, in my view, some of the highest potential for benefit or damage in the body of Christ. I have witnessed prophetic words shared with people, which in an instant completely changed their lives. These changes were most often good, but sometimes they were not good. When anyone opens their mouth and speaks, putting God's name on it, the potential for life change is unlimited.

Coaching also benefits a person's gifting's, spiritual fruit and callings. For example, if someone is too hospitable or misuses mercy, the damage done to themselves and others can normally be turned into something good by a few healthy conversations. Prophecy is another matter entirely. Prophetic people need to receive healthy input and consistent accountability to continually add just the right materials to their lives at just the right time. This will build their character and in turn their prophetic expression. It is easier to learn things the right way the first time than to develop bad habits and have to unlearn things and then re-learn them the right way.

Think of children, they are very easy, or at least fairly easy to work with and train when they are young. But an older person who becomes *set in their ways* can have tremendous difficulty receiving healthy input and an equally difficult time making needed changes in their lives. This is why it is important to take note when those around us begin to express new things. If we have relationship with them or responsibility for them, quickly encourage them in what God is doing in and through them. If there are other people in the church, ministry, or group that are doing the same things, try to connect them and build a strong support group around them. Encourage them to speak with a pastor or leader about this new expression.

Leaders and other trusted people, please take seriously the privilege that God has given us to lovingly and supportively sharpen the gifts/expressions in each other. Be quick to praise and reinforce the good, while gently touching the bad. Might I suggest doing something that my wife does: she calls it the sandwich approach. It looks like this good/growth area/good. This approach is very healthy to reinforce good things while lovingly coaching growth areas. This three-step process looks like this: begin with a genuine complement about something they are doing well. Then discuss something they need to improve a growth area. And then finish up with another genuine complement about something they are doing well. This model works. What it really does is helps us look for the good in others and reinforce it while carefully speaking into growth areas. And since what is being done well is being reinforced, hopefully at least twice as much as growth areas, the people being coached are consistently being transformed in very productive ways.

How many of us want to reach our full potential with God? How many of us want to at the end of our lives hear, "Well done good and faithful servant?" All of us do! But not one of us can do either of these alone. It requires a family. Like the old saying, "It takes a village to raise a child." That pretty much sums up what church groups should look like. We need coaching, accountability, and regular input from those who care about us.

Prophetic people require coaching. I believe this is one of the reasons why many individuals and church groups no longer welcome the prophetic. Many denominations and Church groups have crafted a doctrine that excludes prophecy from our *Now* experience with Christ. This is not accurate Biblically. But giving people a list of do's and don'ts is easier than coaching them and pouring our lives into them.

Remember Peter in the Bible? He was quite prophetic and had a strong personality. He was often the first one to open his mouth and speak. He was also the one the devil asked God for permission to sift. He spoke up on the mount of transfiguration *Matthew 17:4-6*, and Father God *Strongly* coached him. Peter took Jesus to the side and reprimanded Him and Jesus had to rebuke him. -*Matthew 16:22-23*. That was serious coaching. Peter was a handful, as are most fired up, fervent, spirited, Christians. But look how God used Peter!

A few other scriptures on coaching and accountability: Proverbs 10:8, 11:14, 15:31-32, 17:10 19:20, 27:5-6a, 27:9, 27:17, Psalm141:5 & Ecc.7:5.

CHAPTER 5

Prophetic Heart

Devotions and Staying Close to God

God's Father Heart

The Great Facilitator

Devotions and Staying Close to God

Personal devotions and staying close to God are the two most important things we do as Christians.

These include:

- Bible study – See Psalms 119, 1 Peter 2:2-3, Romans 10:17, Ephesians 5:25-26, & John 6:63
- Prayer – Proverbs 15:29, Philippians 4:6, Colossians 4:2, & James 5:16
- Worship-Psalm 29:2, Psalm 95:1, Psalm 95:6, Psalm 95:9, & Psalm 99:5
- Praying in tongues (If you have a prayer language) 1Corinthians 14:2 & vs 15-17, Jude 20, Romans 8:26-27, Ephesians 6:18

I'm sure that as Christians we know the value of Bible study, worship, and prayer. Our time spent with God is the most important part of our life. The more time we spend with our wonderful Lord, the more we love Him. This is also the primary place where we feed upon His word, written or spoken and change things in our lives that hinder us from being more like Jesus.

The Bible describes this beautiful interaction between us and the Holy Spirit. See *Philippians 2:12-14* and *James 1:22-25*. We are changed each day as we spend time with God. The Bible says that we are changed from glory to glory -*2 Corinthian's 3:17-18*. So, the glory that you have in your life today should not be the *same* glory you have in your life next week or next month. The glory spoken of in these verses is a divine quality, Christlikeness. We need to be staying close to God each day and yielding to Holy Spirit's leading in our lives.

Sometimes He will speak very clearly to us through the scripture or sometimes directly into our thoughts. On occasion the Holy Spirit may also speak to us with a sense of a *GO* or *No Go*.

A Go- You just know that it is right, you *feel* good about this or that plan, or decision. You have a sense of peace-filled freedom. You don't fully understand why, but you just know this is the right thing to do or say. It feels like a solid yes *sense* in your spirit.

A No Go- You just don't *feel* right about something, the decision or plan. There's a hesitance in your spirit about it. Something is just wrong with it. You don't fully know what's wrong, but as you think about it, there is no peace or freedom there. This is very much a *no* sense in your spirit. When we sense this *No-Go*, we need to stop for a moment, or as long as needed and ask the Father, "Should I do this or not?" This pausing, waiting and asking God's counsel will give us the answer we need. He may speak to us through any means He chooses. If the hesitancy in our spirit continues through the asking and praying, do not move forward with whatever you were planning. Take more time to pray. Keep in mind that the Holy Spirit is a gentleman. He will not force us to do anything. So, if our mind is made up to go against the *Go or No-Go* sense and we continue to ask God what He thinks while still hoping for a different answer, He will respect our decision and let us do what we want. This *Pushing through His leading* will cause the Holy Spirit to become quiet or quenched in that area.

You may be thinking, "What does this have to do with prophecy?" That's a great question. We need to have consistent devotions and spend ample amounts of time with our God, all the while being careful to listen to His voice and follow His leading.

Our personal life is the primary field that must be purposefully worked if we want God to use us in ever increasing ways. If we do not take our relationship with Him seriously, listening for His voice and doing whatever He says, we have no right to speak for Him prophetically into the lives of others.

May Paul's desire in this verse be ours as well

[10] And this, so that I may know Him [experientially, becoming more thoroughly acquainted with Him, understanding the remarkable wonders of His Person more completely] and [in that same way experience] the power of His resurrection [which overflows and is active in believers], and [that I may share] the fellowship of His sufferings, by being continually conformed [inwardly into His likeness even] to His death [dying as He did]; [11] so that I may attain to the resurrection [that will raise me] from the dead. -Philippians 3:10-11 (AMP)

When we trust Jesus and become part of God's family, the Bible says that we are *joint heirs* with Christ (Ephesians 3), so the riches of our Lord Jesus are also our riches! The Bible speaks of these *riches* in many places. This is just one of the reasons why it is so important that we read and study our Bible and over time know and love the written word. As we read our Bible, there are times the Holy Spirit will illuminate our minds. We will receive a now revelation of the scripture we are reading. This is called the *rhema* or *spoken* word. We all love these precious moments in our devotions when the Holy Spirit opens up the written word *logos* and speaks a now word that we need.

God will often do a very similar thing prophetically. He will share a prophetic word with one of His children that has a scripture base. Meaning, the prophecy is to be shared with a verse or verses of scripture. When a prophetic word is shared together with scripture it forms a beautiful now word for the person who receives it.

The importance of the written word

The written word (scripture) is our solid foundation, so read it, study it, consume it and love it!

God's written word is His will, and we are always to act based on His will. Not the potential outcome. One clear example of this is God's will to heal physically (I Peter 2:24, Psalms 17:20, Matthew 8:17, Proverbs 4:20-23, Proverbs 16:24). These are just a few examples of God's will to heal. When we pray for the sick, is everyone that is prayed for healed? No. Are some healed? Yes. Do we know who will be healed? Sometimes the Holy Spirit shows us, but not always. We still pray for the sick because it is God's will to heal. Being obedient to His will is our responsibility. The outcome is His.

⁶ I planted, Apollos watered, but God [all the while] was causing the growth. ⁷ So neither is the one who plants nor the one who waters anything, but [only] God who causes the growth. ⁸ He who plants and he who waters are one [in importance and esteem, working toward the same purpose]; but each will receive his own reward according to his own labor.
-1 Corinthians 3:6-8 (AMP)

To know His will, we must know His written word

As Paul told Timothy in *2 Timothy 2:15 (Amp.), study and do your best to present yourself to God approved, a workman (tested by trial) who has no reason to be shamed, accurately handling and skillfully teaching the Word of truth.*

The reason that I am strongly encouraging each person who reads this to be a serious student of the Bible is because the written word is the rock that does not change. The Bible is our foundation to build a solid life. The Bible is also the Gold Standard to which every issue in our lives can find a healthy resolution.

All prophecy is subject to the written word. If a prophecy disagrees with the Bible/Scripture, the Bible is always right. The priceless value of the written word for our lives is evident, and an ever increasing knowledge of the Bible is needed to strengthen our prophetic expression.

God's Father Heart

Pursue [this] love [with eagerness, make it your goal], yet earnestly desire and cultivate the spiritual gifts [to be used by believers for the benefit of the church], but especially that you may prophesy [to foretell the future, to speak a new message from God to the people].
-1 Corinthians 14:1 (AMP)

Why would God tell us to seriously, strongly desire spiritual gifts but in particular prophecy? When I first read this, I remember thinking how selfish it would be to go to someone and ask strongly, seriously, and persistently *for a gift*. It just seemed to be selfish. I believe that it is this natural *carnal* view of giving and receiving that causes problems in many Christian's lives.

Let's look at what I call *God's Father Heart*. Throughout the scriptures His true and pure Father heart is seen.

Delight yourself in the Lord, and He will give you the desires and petitions of your heart. -Psalms 37:4 (AMP)

[19] For the Son of God, Jesus Christ, who was preached among you by us, by me, Silvanus, and Timothy, was not "Yes" and "No," but has proved to be "Yes" in Him [true and faithful, the divine "Yes" affirming God's promises]. [20] For as many as are the promises of God, in Christ they are [all answered] "Yes." So through Him we say our "Amen" to the glory of God. -2 Corinthians 1:19-20 (AMP)

[31] But [strive for and actively] seek His kingdom, and these things will be given to you as well. [32] Do not be afraid and anxious, little flock, for it is your Father's good pleasure to give you the kingdom. -Luke 12:31-32 (AMP)

[11]If you then, evil (sinful by nature) as you are, know how to give good and advantageous gifts to your children, how much more will your Father who is in heaven [perfect as He is] give what is good and advantageous to those who keep on asking Him.[12] "So then, in everything treat others the same way you want them to treat you, for this is [the essence of] the Law and the [writings of the] Prophets. -Matthew 7:11-12 (AMP)

Father God longs to be our everything. He gives us all we need to be a strong, healthy and productive Christian. His lavish giving also equips us to strengthen other believers and reach those who do not know Jesus. This is that pure father's heart, always passionately wanting to give us what is best.

But just as it is written [in Scripture]

"Things which the eye has not seen and the ear has not heard,
And which have not entered the heart of man,
All that God has prepared for those who love Him [who hold Him in
affectionate reverence, who obey Him, and who gratefully recognize the
benefits that He has bestowed]."
-1 Corinthians 2:9 (AMP)

My wife and I are parents and grandparents. We both have things we want to give to our family. The things we want to give are not material possessions. They are our love for God, His love for us, His love for them, our knowledge of God, His nature and knowledge of the scriptures. We regularly share our stories of how God came through for us time after time, how much God loves them and life skills. My wife and I want to give these things to our family, friends and others who will continue to pass it on.

This is what Paul's heart was also

The things [the doctrine, the precepts, the admonitions, the sum of my ministry] which you have heard me teach in the presence of many witnesses, entrust [as a treasure] to reliable and faithful men who will also be capable and qualified to teach others. -2 Timothy 2:2 (AMP)

Father God knows that His gifts and abilities are life and world changing. They are always pro-active. Each one, when properly shared, potently expresses God's love and care into the recipient. Every person touched by God directly or through one of His children is changed. Gifts or abilities used lovingly always make Jesus look great! I remember the first prophetic word I received. Afterward, I had this *awe* for God that was greater than I had before. I also started listening for God's voice each day which eventually led to recognizing His voice for me and then He began to speak with me for others as well. All this began on that day when my wife and I received that first prophetic word. That day an expectation was birthed in me. Then, that expectation drove me to study God's written word which confirmed that prophecy is for today. If that wasn't enough, the Bible says all Christians can prophesy. See -I Corinthians 14:31.

The part that takes time is learning to recognize His voice and then knowing what to do with what you hear. God says to us through Paul to desire spiritual gifts, but to especially desire prophecy. I believe Paul was inspired to write this because prophecy, though equal in importance with the other gifts, has at its heart God's desire to clearly communicate with people in certain areas of their lives at just the right moment. God does this so each of us can make the most of our time here (Ephesians 5:16-17). Prophecy sharpens and focuses us. It builds into and upon our relationship with God as well as the specific call on our lives.

The Great Facilitator

Prophecy is also a great facilitator. Here are a few examples of prophetic facilitation:

- Discerning of Spirits reveals that another person is physically ill. The person who receives that information can go and get a person with the gift of healing and return to pray for the person with the physical need.
- If discerning of Spirits reveals a specific call on someone's life, go get someone who is serving in the same or similar area as the call shown to you and introduce them to each other. Share the word and encourage them in the similarity of their call.

Prophecy (future telling) reveals that someone is called to pastor, be an elder, or be in a leadership role, go to the elders/pastor of the church and share the word with them. Then they can pray about the word and the person it was for, and decide what to do next. We do not share words like this with the individual, only share a word like this with leadership. This prophetic word would help facilitate a leader/pastor connection with the person.

There are times when God reveals things to his children that are not to be verbally shared. I have seen this in my life as well as the lives of many others. I have seen this almost too many times to remember.

- God will reveal a specific material need so we can give to the person's specific need at just the right moment.
- He may show us a struggle in someone so we can stand with them in specific prayer. If only we knew how many times God stirred those around us through revelation to pray and lovingly cover us!

God's heart revealed to us does not always require our mouths to express His loving message. It can be by a pat on the back, a smile, a gift of money, food, or any other provision God revealed to us. He reveals this to us so we can give it at just the right time. Prophecy is a great encourager, builder-upper, comforter, facilitator, and on and on. Loving prophecy when shared, produces a healthy fear or *awe* and respect for the Lord. Prophecy also makes relationships even more personal, intimate, and loving.

Testimony

> Prophecy is a great encourager, builder-upper, comforter and facilitator

I will often go into places, stores or markets and ask God to show me people. What He sees in people's lives. I do this in hopes of learning more details of human needs, desires and struggles along with how I can more effectively help others. I also have had many opportunities to encourage others in these places. One time in particular I was standing in the returns line at a store and glancing around, began talking with the Holy Spirit and asking Him to show me things about others' lives. In the midst of this an older man was walking toward the returns line and I asked the Holy Spirit, "What about him?" The Holy Spirit showed me that he and his wife were struggling to take care of their small children. I became puzzled as I looked *discreetly* at this man. He was in his 70's. I thought, "Dana, you must have missed that one." He walked up and stood in line right behind me. I struck up a conversation with Him and to my surprise he began talking of how he and his wife had just gotten custody of their three small grandchildren and were struggling to take care of them at their older age. I then was able to speak encouragement to him based on the revelation that the Lord had given me. Wow! You go, God! God's Father Heart is to give and keep on giving, to love and keep on loving!

CHAPTER 6

Prophetic Keys

The Power of Expectation

Fertile Environment

The Power of Expectation

All of us want a better quality of life. In fact, expectation is what caused each of us to choose Jesus as our Lord. We each knew the life we had, and by revelation of the Holy Spirit believed that Jesus was the only way to have a better one. This is the moment in each person's heart where the evidence is presented clearly enough to make the right decision. Like in a court room, we have our *Natural life* before Christ on one side (the prosecution), and on the other side of the room we have the defense (Jesus) saying, Trust me and you will be forgiven and have a better quality of life now and forever. Romans 2:4 says that God's goodness leads us to think differently (make good decisions). Christians, not one of us would have chosen Jesus if we did not expect a better life.

Expectations are a very powerful! Expectation led us to choose Christ, they help us to make good decisions, and if we are not careful they can also get us into some really big messes! Expectation is very important to the Holy Spirit. He will meet us in our God focused expectations every time. He may not always give us what we want, but He will always meet us there.

But as for me, I will look expectantly for the Lord and with confidence in Him I will keep watch; I will wait [with confident expectation] for the God of my salvation. My God will hear me. -Micah 7:7 (AMP)

When we wait on the Lord, we do this out of expectancy. If we did not believe that our God loves us dearly and that He will help us and meet our needs, we would not expect anything from Him.

Let's look at what happened when the people of Nazareth expected nothing from Jesus:

¹Jesus left there and came to His hometown [Nazareth]; and His disciples followed Him. ² When the Sabbath came, He began to teach in the synagogue; and many who listened to Him were astonished, saying, "Where did this man get these things [this knowledge and spiritual insight]? What is this wisdom [this confident understanding of the Scripture] that has been given to Him, and such miracles as these performed by His hands?³ Is this not the carpenter, the son of Mary, and the brother of James and Joses and Judas and Simon? Are His sisters not here with us?" And they were [deeply] offended by Him [and their disapproval blinded them to the fact that He was anointed by God as the Messiah]. ⁴Jesus said to them, "A prophet is not without honor (respect) except in his hometown and among his relatives and in his own household."⁵ And He could not do a miracle there at all [because of their unbelief] except that He laid His hands on a few sick people and healed them.⁶ He wondered at their unbelief. And He was going around in the villages teaching. -Mark 6:1-6 (AMP)

In these verses, we see Jesus teaching in the church. The people were looking at Him but did not see God in Him. All they saw was a local man who was just like them. They knew His family and did not believe in Him. As such, they did not connect with God expecting good things. In verse 5 it says that Jesus was not able to bless many people there because of their unbelief. Just as Jesus could not minister effectively to these people, this can happen with us too. I have had instances where I knew God wanted to bless someone. The Holy Spirit would point them out and I knew God wanted to share something with them, but as soon as I approached them to share a word, the Holy Spirit withdrew and the prophetic anointing quickly disappeared.

I could feel the Holy Spirit being quenched. The first time this happened I was startled. I started searching my heart and asking the Holy Spirit questions. I thought something was wrong with me. Had I upset him? Was my motive off? What could I have done different? I was quite upset. That is when the Holy Spirit shared with me the scripture that we just looked at of Jesus in his hometown. Then the Holy Spirit shared with me about the power of healthy expectation.

We can be full of faith and the Holy Spirit, have a prophetic word, or other gifting stirring in us for someone and be ready to share it. But, if the other person does not see God in our lives and draw on Him, there will not be that beautiful healthy exchange God desires. So, do not beat yourself up if a ministry interaction with someone is strange or unusually unproductive. It is always a good idea to connect with God and ask Him questions when something unusual happens. But, I will say this one more time, "Don't beat yourself up." These are great Q

> Do not beat yourself up if a ministry interaction with someone is strange or unusually unproductive

& A and teaching moments for us and the Holy Spirit. He loves to teach us, coach us and lead us into all truth.

Fertile Environment

When we prophesy, we are like a gardener sowing seed. We want the spoken word to find fertile ground in the person's life and bear much fruit for Jesus. Good gardeners do much more than walk out to the garden spot and randomly throw the seeds, walk away, and expect a huge harvest. God's word is seed. His written word, the *Bible,* is the best seed there is. Prophecy, *His spoken word,* is great seed also.

Keep this gardening analogy in mind...

Sharing a prophetic word is like planting a seed. There is a need to be thoughtful of the ground, *those who will hear the message,* before you plant or *share* the message.

We don't plant in winter when it is snowing. An example of trying to plant in winter would be receiving a prophetic word and sharing it with your pastor 10 minutes before they are speaking. Now, an encouragement such as "You are right on track," "God is pleased with you," or "I believe you have the word in season today," could be very helpful to pastors and leaders in their speaking and planning. If God gives you an encouragement like these, it would be seed in springtime to your pastor. But a word that required their mind to disengage from their message and go somewhere completely different would be inappropriate here.

Also, be sensitive to what is going on in a person's life. Such as commitments like having to be at work in five minutes or a sick child. You get the picture. Try to plant in springtime as often as possible. For instance, if you have a word for the pastor, connect with them after they are done sharing and let them know you have a word for them. Then plan a time to share the word. In the case of the friend racing off to work, you could send a text and set up a visit some other time. It is better not to be rushed when giving or receiving prophecy. I understand that most everyone is busy. What I am going for here is an awareness of timing. Try as much as possible to see or create those springtime moments to plant the seed.

> When we really value a person and genuinely care about them, they know it

Like apples of gold in settings of silver
is a word spoken at the right time.
-Proverbs 25:11 (AMP)

Respecting and honoring others is a huge part of creating a fertile environment for sharing a word. Many people have been hurt, offended, taken advantage of or just rubbed wrong by someone. In this life being humble and showing *genuine* respect and honor to someone will make more difference to create a springtime setting than almost anything else. When we really value a person and genuinely care about them, they know it. If someone senses that we are just *getting our ministry on*, they will know that as well. Our goal as God's representatives is to do our very best to help people open up to God and grant Him deeper access to the soil of their heart.

The entrance of your words gives light.
–Psalm 119:130a (WEB)

Entrance here means opening or unfurling. When we open our mouth, we must be deliberate with what unfolds from our lips. Care and love will help people stay open and receptive longer and they will allow deeper access to the soil of their heart. However, if we are perceived as uncaring or pushy they will close down quickly.

It is always appropriate to be nice

Pleasant words are a honeycomb,
Sweet to the soul and healing to the bones.
-Proverbs 16:24 (NASB)

When we speak pleasant words, people respond with a desire to hear more. Then the access to the soil stays open longer. Being kind and respectful to others honors God. It also helps reinforce and strengthen the person throughout our whole interaction with them.

I have a saying, "It is always appropriate to be nice." Treat others with kindness and respect. Love unconditionally, visibly, and tangibly prefer others. Be obedient to God and look for the best time and method to share prophetic words with others.

CHAPTER 7

The Flesh and the Spirit

Relationship, God's First Priority

The Flesh and The Spirit

There is a war in every Christian. On one side there is the Holy Spirit and our spirit. On the other side is our soul. Simply put, it is a battle between good and bad, light and dark, selflessness and selfishness. See Galatians 5:16-18. Also, look at how clearly Paul explains it in Romans 7:14-25. This ongoing battle that each one of us works through is the process of sanctification: Our day to day partnering with the Holy Spirit to drive out our selfish nature. This selfish nature expresses itself the same in each of us as it did in the one we all received it from. Namely, Adam. *Romans 5:12-21.* Adam received it from Satan when he disobeyed God and chose to listen to him instead. We see selfishness modeled by the originator himself. Satan.

> [13] *"But you said in your heart,*
> *'I will ascend to heaven;*
> *I will raise my throne above the stars of God;*

I will sit on the mount of assembly
In the remote parts of the north.
¹⁴ 'I will ascend above the heights of the clouds;
I will make myself like the Most High.'
-Isaiah 14:13-14 (AMP)

Here is a small list of the I wills. Please check your heart to see if you have any I wills that need to die:

I will look good

I will fix them

I will share my opinions

I will do a better job than they are

If they would only listen to me I will help them

I will _____

This is the opposite of trusting God. The statements above definitely do not prefer others. So let's tie this in with prophecy. If we believe God has spoken to us and we have a prophetic word for someone, there must be a God led carefulness in us, a peace-filled caution, a thorough process of seeing and considering the word, loving and preferring others and sensing and physically watching for the best setting and time to deliver the word. And in all this, keeping our fleshly nature subject to the Holy Spirit.

I know this is a lot to consider. But if you will build these processes into your life, over time, they will become a part of you. They will no longer be something you do. They will become who you are. We are to *do it until we become it.*

Thoughts

The Bible says we are to take every thought captive to the obedience of Jesus, making the thoughts that are selfish, unhealthy, or destructive subject to the Lordship of Jesus.

We are destroying sophisticated arguments and every exalted and proud thing that sets itself up against the [true] knowledge of God, and we are taking every thought and purpose captive to the obedience of Christ,
-2 Corinthians 10:5 (AMP)

The importance of consistently being able to take every thought captive when prophesying is seen here:

[31] For [in this way] you can all prophesy one by one, so that everyone may be instructed and everyone may be encouraged; [32] for the spirits of prophets are subject to the prophets [the prophecy is under the speaker's control, and he can stop speaking]; [33] for God [who is the source of their prophesying] is not a God of confusion and disorder but of peace and order. -1 Corinthian's 14:31-33 (AMP)

Paul says that we can all prophesy one by one, and in verse 32 it says that "The spirit of the prophet is subject to the prophet." Meaning, when we have a word from God to share, we choose when to speak, what to speak and we choose how much or how long to speak.

The purity of God's revelation will challenge the impurities of the human delivery vessel (us). I regularly question my motives and examine my heart's purity before the Lord. The significance of being His representative is overwhelming considering all my flaws. So, please take seriously the reality of this battle in each of us. Love God and people more than anything else. More than expressing any gift. More than fulfilling your call. More than achieving any goal. Let the love of God be *more* in everything. Overwhelming love overwhelms the *I will* in us every time.

Relationship, God's First Priority

Our God loves each one of us so very much. In fact, He values our relationship with Him above all else. That's why Jesus came and died. Father God's desire for intimacy with us is His first priority, and as such, He will go to extreme lengths to maintain the relationship. Knowing this presents each Christian with a tremendous responsibility to be as sure as possible that we are not simply "Hearing what we want to hear".

Read the following scripture: Numbers 22:1-35. In these verses Balak the king of Moab is very afraid of the people of Israel so he sends the elders of Moab and Midian to hire a prophet named Balaam to come and curse the Israelites. The messengers arrive and share the king's request with him. Balaam listens to their request, then, he asks the messengers to spend the night. Balaam then prays and talks with the Lord to see what he should do. In 22:9-12 God comes and visits him. They talk and God tells Balaam, "You shall not go with them." –Numbers 22:12a. The next morning Balaam sends the messengers away. Then, King Balak sends another group to Balaam with the same request. Balaam asks this group to stay the night as well and in verse 19 he indicates that he wants God to tell him something more (i.e. different) than what God said to him the first time. In verse 20 God tells Balaam to go with the men. Did God change His mind? No, He didn't. In verse 22 God was angry that Balaam went and God stands on the path with a sword blocking his way. Balaam cannot see God blocking his path. But, his donkey sure does and veers off the path to avoid death. Balaam strikes the donkey and keeps on going. God blocks Balaam 3 times and every time, Balaam strikes the donkey and continues on. In verse 28 the Lord lets the donkey speak to Balaam. In verse 29 Balaam blames his donkey for hindering his progress. Then, in verse 31 God opens Balaam's eyes and he sees God blocking his way, opposing him. God says to Balaam in verse 32 that he is acting "Perverse or Contrary" to Him. You can see this perverseness again in verse 34 when Balaam tells God that if what he is doing is evil, he will stop it. God again tells him to keep on going to King Balak.

Why would God tell Balaam not to go and then tell him to go? Then, act as if He was going to kill him, but, not really want to kill him? Why would God then let the donkey see Him so that Balaam would not die? God opposed Balaam's plan 3 times. And if that was not clear enough, God initiates a conversation between Balaam and his donkey. Then, God speaks to him and when He sees that Balaam is still determined to go. He tells him to keep on going.

Now let's revisit our topic in light of these scriptures. Father God desires relationship above all else. Above anything we will ever do or not do. Our loving Father God will always respect our choices. If we choose to do something out of His will or plan for us He will respect that also. God spoke with Balaam and shared His will with him. However, Balaam did not like God's plan. He *reasoned* his way through it. He preferred his own plan. Then, we see God telling Balaam what he *Wanted* to hear. With this in mind, please remember that each one of us has the potential to choose our own plans and desires over God's. If that happens like it did with Balaam, God, because of His great love and desire to save the relationship, could begin to speak *what we want to hear*. If we persist in disobeying God, He may eventually stop trying to get us back on track. This is very much like quenching the Holy Spirit. Father God is not going to argue with us in prayer over our will. He is far too kind and loves us to much to interfere with our free will.

Please note: I am not saying that a person will *lose* their salvation. I am saying that they could lose their intimacy with God.

CHAPTER 8

Don't Prophesy Your Word

To Someone Else

Don't Prophesy Your Word to Someone Else

A few years ago, my wife and I were training a group of people in the prophetic. There was a young man participating in the training that had things going on in his life that he and the Holy Spirit were working through. He had shared much of this with me before the class began. As the group progressed from learning to recognize God's voice, to hearing from God for others and finally sharing revelation with others, I noticed the words the young man shared with others were very specific to his *own situation*. In fact, they were great words that spoke to what God was doing in his own life. I watched him do this three times with three different people. He was clearly hearing God's voice and interpreting the revelation accurately. The words were just not for others. They were for him. That is when I took him to the side and we discussed what he was doing.

When we believe that God has given us prophetic revelation, if it fits our situation and connects with us in a specific or personal way that causes us to feel hope and encouragement in our heart or it could be similar to other prophetic words that we have received, pause and ask God, "Is this for me?" This can be sorted out pretty quickly when we are alone and revelation comes without a clear recipient coming to mind. However, in a group or while ministering to someone else, this can require a little more sorting out. This is an encouragement to all of us, as God is working in each one of our lives

Example

I recently had a prophecy for another person. The Lord showed me this man and his wife discussing their future, the next leg of the race. They were looking at finances and desiring to spend more time together. I heard the Lord say that he was going to give them wisdom as they work through these plans. I pondered this word for several minutes before sharing it, as my wife and I were in exactly the same place. When the Lord showed me the man and his wife, I could see their faces. But, I still paused before sharing because the word so accurately fit my current circumstances. I also clearly sensed the Holy Spirit wanted me to share the word with him, but I take the prophetic seriously. Knowing that when I open my mouth and put God's name on it, I need to be as sure as possible that what I speak has with all that is in me been examined, and ran through all of the God-given filters and wisdom that I have at that very moment. I have found that genuine love and care for other people's lives and their well-being is the filter that best sifts the words I share with others. I did share the word with the other man and he confirmed that it was accurate by promptly agreeing with it.

So, if you receive revelation that really fits your life and ministers to your needs, pause briefly and ask God questions to make sure that the word lovingly connects with the right person. Whether you or some other blessed person!

CHAPTER 9

Gaps and Walls

Gaps and Walls

The prophet Ezekiel was used by God to share a picture of prophecy.

⁴ O Israel, your prophets have been like foxes among the ruins. 5 You have not gone up into the gaps or breaches, nor built the wall around the house of Israel that it might stand in the battle on the day of the Lord. -Ezekiel 13:4-5 (AMP)

This scripture says what the prophets have not done. Meaning that this is what they should have done. All of our lives are like a wall, and each person has gaps or *breaches* in their walls. Prophecy speaks to people for their building up, encouragement, and comfort. -1 Corinthians 14:3. What prophecy does is speak exactly what a person needs at just the right time into the gaps in their life. The Bible consistently builds our entire life, adding strength and life to every area. But each of us has gaps that are a result of many things. A few of which are hurt, disappointment, family of origin issues, sins and even the call on our lives will reveal and often create gaps. Gaps are also exposed as we are being transformed and purified by the Holy Spirit. Gaps are places in our life that need to connect with God.

Look back at Ezekiel 13:5 again. It says that we, *prophetic people*, are to go up into the gaps. Meaning, we need to deliberately position ourselves in others' lives and help them connect with God right where needed. We also need others to do the same for us. Let's look at another verse that shows us what this going up into the gaps looks like.

[28] Her prophets have smeared whitewash for them, seeing false visions and divining lies for them, saying, 'Thus says the Lord God'—when the Lord has not spoken. [29] The people of the land have practiced oppression and extortion and have committed robbery; they have wronged the poor and needy and they have oppressed the stranger without justice. [30] I searched for a man among them who would build up the wall and stand in the gap before Me for [the sake of] the land, that I would not destroy it, but I found no one [not even one]. -Ezekiel 22:28-30(AMP)

Here again, the subject of prophecy is being spoken of. False prophecy in verse 28, and then in verse 29 it speaks of the gaps in the lives of the people of the land. In verse 30, God says through the prophet that He looked for a man among them, *the prophets*, who would take responsibility for others well-being and deliberately invest in others' lives. They were to do this by lovingly positioning themselves between the people and God; interceding and standing in the gaps. Those areas that needed to connect with God. And crying out in love for the people just as Moses did in Psalm 106:23. Moses interceded for the people of Israel many times. I believe that as we love our neighbor as we love ourselves and pray and seek God for them, we are choosing to step into these gaps and strengthen their lives. Very often in that intercessory position, we will hear God's heart and plans for them.

For several years I sensed there was something more to the prayer/prophecy connection that I just didn't understand. A few years ago this truth finally cleared up as I read these and other scriptures. I believe that to consistently and lovingly prophesy, we must have the heart of an intercessor. We are to be people of prayer, individuals who love others so much that we look for and take seriously our role as *gap filler* for others. We must want God's best for those around us, praying without ceasing, and constantly looking for opportunities to encourage people. We need to have the mindset of a soldier, and be quick to fight in the spirit for others well-being.

Looking back at Ezekiel chapter 13 verse 5 again; it speaks of people standing in the battle on the day of the Lord. The Bible says in Ephesians 6 verse 12 that our battle is not against flesh and blood (people) but against demonic forces. Christians, our fight is never with another person. In Ezekiel, I believe the battle spoken of is referring to the days in each of our lives when the Lord Jesus is taking ground. The ground that is not yet fully yielded to His Lordship; such as selfishness, wrong motives, negative traditions, and wrong mindsets. These are the enemies of the Lord that we need God's help and His perspective to overcome. The devil does everything within his power to keep these areas of our lives unchanged and independent of Jesus' lordship. These battles for purity and holiness happen in each of us. Only the overall life strengthening power of God's written word, prayer, and worship, along with the specific gap filling, strengthening nature of prophecy can give us the power to stand strong in the midst of anything. God meets us right where we are and gives us the word we need at just the right moment. *Proverbs 15:23 & 25:11* Prophecy helps so much to connect people with God and then He helps each of us to overcome the gaps in our lives.

Prophetic Intercession

An example from my wife, Cheryl

A friend asked me to pray for their adult son. I cared deeply for him so I began praying for him daily. After about a week, he simply stopped coming to mind. While working at a restaurant that weekend, I thought I saw this young man across the room. I looked again and it was not him. Then, I saw him again across the room. This happened about four or five more times. I would *see* him out of the corner of my eye or at a glance and I would feel startled. Of course, when I thought about it, I knew he would not be at the restaurant with me as we live 600 miles apart. This happened the next night I worked as well. Only this time I asked God, "Are you trying to tell me something?"

I began to pray and felt strongly that God did not want me to stop praying for this young man. I sensed that I was to continue to intercede for him. I prayed daily for him and after a few more weeks, I lost the sense of urgency to pray again. I asked God, "Is he ok? Do I need to keep praying?" Immediately, I got a picture of him experiencing healing and breakthrough. I had no way of knowing for sure so I kept praying until I had the opportunity to check on him. About a week and a half later, my friend told me he was doing much better. He had started feeling better at about the same time I felt the need to pray diminish. God kept me in tune with what He was doing and I was able to stay more connected with my friend through the difficult season.

There are many times in all of our lives where just we and God must work through things. There are also other times where God will use other caring people to speak into our lives. Cultivate the role of intercessor (prayerfully and prophetically) in your life by positioning yourself in the gaps of the lives that God has so kindly placed around you.

Extras

Sample Church protocol for visitors who will be preaching, teaching or ministering

Sample Church Leadership protocol for a submitted prophetic word

Biblical Guidelines for leaders when a prophetic word is submitted

Sample protocol for visitors who will be preaching, teaching or ministering

We, the leadership, place the utmost importance on caring for and providing a safe place for those ministering and those who receive ministry. Therefore, if you believe God has given you a prophetic word for someone, please adhere to the following scriptural guidelines:

But [on the other hand] the one who prophesies speaks to people for edification [to promote their spiritual growth] and [speaks words of] encouragement [to uphold and advise them concerning the matters of God] and [speaks words of] consolation [to compassionately comfort them].
- I Corinthians 14:3 (AMP)

We ask that anything beyond the scope of these guidelines be shared with the Leadership before speaking directly with the person with whom you would like to speak.

The following are a few examples of words that need to be shared with the leadership before sharing with others:

Directional Words: Words that speak about calls to ministry, relocation, major life changes, negative things, or job/ministry changes. Words that tell the person to do something (this is giving the speaker undue influence in directing another person's life).

Correctional Words: Words that lovingly share a better way of doing something. These could also be words that point out another person's flaws, sin, or trying to fix someone. These types of words require stewarding between the leaders and the person receiving the word.

Dates: Specific dates or a specific time frame within which something will happen. Examples include: saying that a trial/season of life will be over in six months or you will have a job change by the end of the year. This type of word creates a timeline that God will have to fulfill. This will lead to an unhealthy expectation on the Lord and also the leaders around the person who received the word.

Mates: Matchmaking. Predicting spouses, divorces, or connecting people into relationship with each other.

If you have questions about Prophetic Ministry Protocols at _____ Ministry/ church, we would be happy to visit with you. Thank you for joining us in the work here.

Sample Church Leadership protocol for a submitted prophetic word

The following types of Prophetic words should be submitted to leaders before they are shared with other individuals:

Directional words: These are words that tell someone to do something, go somewhere, or make a significant change in their lives.

Examples include:

Start pastoring / ministering, change jobs/careers, relocate, leave their church, etc.

These words require much prayer and stewarding/support between the person who the word is for, the leaders, family & close friends around them. Church/group leaders must prayerfully consider these types of words, determining that they are accurate before they can be shared with the individual.

Correctional words:

Correctional words are rare, but occasionally happen and must also be carefully, prayerfully considered before sharing with an individual. A God given correctional word will always have a theme of love, hope and restoration while also showing a better way. If a correctional word is submitted to leadership that is hard or harsh, *Fixing someone* without that *Fathers Heart* of love should be viewed as inaccurate.

[11] For the Scripture says, "Whoever believes in Him will not be [a]disappointed."(Lit. put to shame) -Romans 10:11 (NASB)

Or do you have no regard for the wealth of His kindness and tolerance and patience [in withholding His wrath]? Are you [actually] unaware or ignorant [of the fact] that God's kindness leads you to repentance [that is, to change your inner self, your old way of thinking—seek His purpose for your life]? -Romans 2:4 (AMP)

Biblical Guidelines for leaders when a prophetic word is submitted

[16] Rejoice always and delight in your faith; [17] be unceasing and persistent in prayer; [18] in every situation [no matter what the circumstances] be thankful and continually give thanks to God; for this is the will of God for you in Christ Jesus. [19] Do not quench [subdue, or be unresponsive to the working and guidance of] the [Holy] Spirit. [20] Do not scorn or reject gifts of prophecy or prophecies [spoken revelations—words of instruction or exhortation or warning]. [21] But test all things carefully [so you can recognize what is good]. Hold firmly to that which is good. [22] Abstain from every form of evil [withdraw and keep away from it]. -I Thess. 5:16-22 (Amp)

As we certainly want the Holy Spirit to freely move in everyone's life, and speak to us personally and prophetically, we must as in verse 21 "test" what is said. Leaders must prayerfully consider words submitted. They should also discuss the words with other leaders that have responsibility for the person that the word is for. There is a special grace on leaders to discern the heart of God for people under their care.

God also shares these *types* of words with plenty of time for the leaders to judge and weigh the words. As it says in I Thess. 5:21. Keep what is good. There are times when certain *parts* of a prophecy are good and other parts are not good. This prayerful *weighing* and careful discussion with other leaders will *sift* the word and separate the good from the bad (vs 22).

A note on *weighing* a word: As you are prayerfully considering a prophetic word, if it is from God, it will have what I call staying power. The word will remain strong under the closest scrutiny or examination. Human words or satanic words will begin to wither and lose potency. If after prayer and discussion, the leader team does not have peace with the submitted word, it should not be shared with the individual.

If there are *parts* of the word that the leaders feel good about, share only the good and let the rest go. If any part of the word disagrees with the Bible, the written Word of God, it is inaccurate.

Helpful Scriptures for consideration in this process

Proverbs 11:14, 15:22, 24:6, & I Corinthians 14:29-33

Beloved, do not believe every spirit [speaking through a self-proclaimed prophet]; instead test the spirits to see whether they are from God, because many false prophets and teachers have gone out into the world.
-I John 4:1 (AMP)

The word *test* here means to test, examine, prove and scrutinize. If there is agreement among the leaders that the *word* should be shared, consider who and how the word will be given. Should it be shared with the person by the leader team (the group), with a particular leader being the one speaking or by one leader personally representing the team? It may be that a particular leader has a stronger relationship with the individual and would be the best person to share with them. Also, the sensitive nature of the word or content will play into who is present when the word is shared. Doing all things in love and respect will have the best outcome.

For more information contact Dana at:

2danaeast@gmail.com

Dana and his wife Cheryl offer

-Prophetic Seminars

-Prophetic Ministry/Presbytery meetings for individual or groups

-Help for church's or groups to establish healthy prophetic teams *in house* with continued coaching support for them after the teams are established

-Speaking, teaching and preaching

Made in the USA
Middletown, DE
24 February 2022